D0767216

A FRIEND FOR LIFE

The Story
of
Katie Mackinnon

Presented to

Claire MacSween
for
Diligence and
Attendance

C.L.C. Bookshops.

© 1991 Katie Mackinnon & Linda Neilands
ISBN 1 871 676 789

Published by
Christian Focus Publications Ltd.
Geanies House, Fearn, Ross-shire,
IV20 1TW, Scotland, U.K.

Printed and bound in Great Britain
by Cox & Wyman Ltd, Reading

Cover illustration
by
Mike Taylor

Cover design
by
Seoris McGillivray

CONTENTS

1
TUMMY TROUBLE

Katie Ann MacKinnon skipped down the path of her farmhouse home, her happiness growing with every step. Yes, this was the way to spend a bright spring morning - out in the open air, not cooped up in a stuffy class-room with her school-mates.

The gypsy encampment was almost in sight. A few more skips, and there it was, transforming the grassy space of the bottom field into a fair-ground-like hive of activity. It happened the same way every Spring. The gypsies would trail up from the ferry, weighed down under their huge bundles and set up camp on her father's land.

Katie stared at the colourful scene - the dogs, the barefooted children, the scattering of tunnel-shaped tents. Soon the women would be crossing the fields to her door, opening their enormous bundles and trying to persuade her mum to buy their wares: hair slides, skirts, safety pins, pot scrubbers. There seemed no end to the variety of things they carried around. Imagine moving about like that all the time, the girl marvelled.

Her family had only ever moved once - from their thatched croft on the island of Skye to the big old farmhouse on Mull. Her dad had hired a boat for the day and she and her sister had sat between upturned tables and chairs, watching the seagulls swooping and diving into the sea. Of course moving wasn't such a major operation if you were a gypsy. Gypsies didn't believe in cluttering their tents with stuff.

With a slight sense of envy the girl continued on her way, skirting the side of the hazel wood until she reached the river. There was no bridge, but that didn't matter. Surefooted, she jumped from the flat surface of one stepping-stone to the next, pausing midway to dabble a hand in the water and watch for the silver flash of a minnow. Then, hop, hop, hop, she had arrived.

Three pair of large liquid eyes observed her approach. Her father's cows stood like statues in the mud. 'Milking-time. Come on, then.' With a swish of her hazel switch Katie urged them into action.

She didn't rush the journey back. The cows were content to amble along and Katie wanted to drain the last drop of satisfaction from her trip. Her mind was still on the gypsies and the gypsy children who helped their parents by gathering firewood from around their encampment and carrying water from the river. This morning she was helping her parents too.

Her dad was waiting outside the farmhouse when she finally drove the cows into the yard.

'I'm back, Dad,' she called brightly.

He answered with a frown.

Oh dear! She was in trouble. She sensed it even before he spoke. What's more - she knew why. With a horrible sinking feeling in her stomach she slipped past him into the kitchen.

Her mum stood peeling potatoes at the sink. Katie greeted her with an anxious babble of words.

'I'm feeling great now, Mum. Much better. It must have been the walk. The pain's completely gone.'

'The pain was never there,' her father's voice interrupted. He had followed her through the doorway - a fiercely impressive figure in his working boots and leggings. 'That whole noise you made this morning - all about nothing. What you wanted was a day off school and your mum was soft enough to believe you.'

Katie hung her head, totally ashamed. She hadn't meant to deceive her mum and dad - it had just seemed such a great idea, complaining of a pain in her tummy and being allowed to stay at home. Her mum needed a hand after all. And even though housework was right at the bottom of Katie's list of favourite activities, anything had seemed better than a test in English grammar. But now instead of being praised for her helpfulness, she was being scolded.

It always seemed to turn out that way, the girl

thought as she trailed upstairs in disgrace. Time and again her helpfulness went wrong. Her mind drifted over a few examples: the time at her granny's when she'd been told not to touch the churn. She'd wanted so very badly to help make the butter. How was she to know that her first turn of the handle would send cream spattering all over the ceiling!

And then there was the time she'd sent her baby sister hurtling over a bank at the bottom of a hill. 'I told you not to touch that pram. The child might have been killed,' her mother had raged. But Katie had only wanted to take baby Rona for a walk. She had felt exactly the same then as she felt now. Sorry. Guilty. Confused. Why was it she always ended up being bad, no matter how much she intended to be good?

It was years before she found an answer to that question - years, in fact before she even suspected that an answer might exist. She knew she didn't enjoy the feeling of being a bad girl. She just thought it was something she had to put up with because that was the way she'd been born.

From that day on, though, she gave up pretending to have tummy-ache. Tests or no tests, she was outside the house with her sisters every morning waiting for the big black school car to pick them up.

What a shock, then, to wake up one morning

and feel a real pain stabbing like a bread-knife in her side.

'Mum, I don't feel well,' she wailed, tossing and turning in the bed.

This time there was no talk of sending her out to fetch cows.

The doctor came. 'Acute appendicitis,' he pronounced after carefully pressing her tummy. 'I'll arrange for the lassie to be admitted to Oban Cottage Hospital.'

At that Katie felt more miserable than ever. It was bad enough to be so sick, but to have to leave the island and stay in a strange hospital without her mum seemed too hard to bear.

'Don't leave me, Mum. I'm so afraid,' she sobbed as the arrangements were made.

'I'll write to you, love. We all will.' Mrs. MacKinnon wasn't the sort of mother to make a show of her emotions but Katie could see she was upset. 'And listen, I'm going to teach you something that will help you be brave.'

The promised talisman turned out to be the twenty-third psalm. All the way to Oban Katie's mum went over the words again and again, until by the time they reached the hospital the girl knew every sentence off by heart.

'Just you keep saying it. Everything will be all right.' Mrs. MacKinnon planted a parting kiss on her daughter's cheek.

'The Lord is my shepherd...The Lord is my shepherd...' Katie could feel her panic rising as she lay alone in her hospital bed. 'The Lord is my shepherd.' It was no good. No matter how often she claimed the Lord was her shepherd, deep down she pictured him more as an angry schoolmaster, as likely to punish her as keep her safe.

'Now then, who have we here? Katie, is it? Well, I'm Nurse MacKenzie. Why are you crying, pet?'

The girl looked up through her tears and saw a white-uniformed nurse by her bed.

'I'm crying because I want to stay at home with my mummy,' she gulped.

'Of course you do,' Nurse MacKenzie smiled and patted her hand. 'But while you're in hospital let's just pretend that I'm your mummy, or maybe your friend - whatever you like. And every day I'll be here to look after you until you're able to go home to your real mummy again.'

Katie sniffed and wiped her eyes. 'Will you be here when I wake up from my operation?'

'I most certainly will,' her new friend smiled.

From that moment on, Katie began to cheer up. Being in hospital wasn't so bad after all. Although her tummy was still very sore for a day or two after she came back from theatre, she had stopped feeling lonely. The doctors made her laugh. Nurse MacKenzie knew exactly how to make her comfortable, and she had never had so many cards and letters and visitors in her life.

Still once she felt better, she couldn't help wondering what she was going to do for the rest of her stay. I'm going to get very bored, she thought to herself. But she was wrong.

Early one morning a wooden cot was put up right beside Katie's bed. A couple of hours later, to her very great delight, it had an occupant - a cuddly, downy-haired baby.

Katie loved babies. At home she was used to being surrounded by baby animals - lambs, calves, kittens, puppies. She had even become an expert at feeding drops of milk to baby rabbits through a hollow dandelion stalk. But human babies were a hundred times more interesting; and here was a lovely little baby boy lying so close to her bed she could watch every single thing he did.

Johnny was the baby's name. And very soon it became understood that Katie was helping Nurse MacKenzie to look after him. When the time came for Johnny's feed, it was Katie who held the feeding bottle. When Johnny started to pull his legs up and roar, it was Katie who let Nurse MacKenzie know there was a problem. The days flew past after that. Looking after Johnny kept her so busy and so happy she never even glanced at the clock.

All the same it was a very wonderful moment

when a dear familiar figure finally appeared in the ward doorway. 'Mum!' Katie flew from her bed and flung her arms around her mother.

'You've a grand lassie there, Mrs. MacKinnon,' Nurse MacKenzie smiled, 'She's been a real help on the ward. We're going to miss her.'

Back home at last, Katie quickly felt as if she'd never been away. Of course there was a welcome home party, with scones and oatcake and all her favourite things to eat. But after a few days of special treatment, back she went to school. One thing had changed, though. Having her appendix out had helped her to make a very important decision. She had an answer now for anyone who asked her what she wanted to be when she grew up. Without a moment's hesitation she would reply: 'A nurse.'

2
ON THE WARDS

At last the day came. Brrring, the alarm clock rang shrilly at six o'clock. Katie was already wide-awake, full of excitement. Today was her first day on the wards. After two years in pre-nursing school and a six week pre-training course, she was about to start caring for real live patients on the children's ward of the Royal Northern Infirmary in Inverness!

How carefully she dressed - smoothing every crease from her uniform, pinning up her hair so that not a single dark wisp escaped from under her cap, firmly lacing her snug-fitting flat-heeled shoes. She was determined to look her best, to do her best, to be the very best nurse she possibly could.

Bang on time she reported to the Ward Sister for duty. From that moment until she was finally dismissed at six o'clock that evening, she was never off her feet. 'Fill this', 'Empty that', 'Scrub this', 'Help with that','Measure this', 'Record that'. She obeyed a never-ending flow of instructions.

Whew! Eight hours later she collapsed in an armchair in the nurses' wing. Her feet felt as if they were about to explode. 'I don't think my toes will ever recover,' she moaned to a fellow-student, who had just limped into the room.

At least she wasn't alone in her exhaustion. That was one of the good things about being part of a group all starting together. Already she had made some particular friends. There was tall thin Ishbel, pretty blond Belle, warm-hearted Ann. And then, there was Jenny.

Jenny was Katie's room-mate. The two of them got on well, but right from their first evening together Katie had realized that their attitudes to nursing were completely different. 'I'll be hopeless. I know it. I only filled in the application form because Mum made me,' Jenny had confided. And now, even though every-one was complaining, her roommate seemed to have had the hardest time of all. 'It was awful. I kept getting mixed up and dropping things and the Sister looked crosser and crosser,' she wailed. 'If it hadn't been my first day, I'd probably have ended up in Matron's office.'

'No, you wouldn't. Sisters always look like they've swallowed vinegar. It must be written into their terms of employment,' Katie tried to reassure her.

At the same time she couldn't help wondering if Jenny would make the grade. The Sister Tutor had left them in no doubt that the very highest standards would be demanded and Jenny seemed so convinced she was going to fail.

As far as Katie was concerned the idea of failure never entered her head. She might moan about her throbbing toes, but underneath she had loved every minute of her working day. Even the washing, scrubbing and polishing had given her a thrill. It had all seemed so worthwhile, keeping things spotless for the sake of the patients. Yes, her first taste of real live nursing had left her more certain than ever that this was the job for her.

Her enthusiasm continued throughout the whole of those gruelling first weeks. (The idea seemed to be that first year student nurses needed to be landed with all the nastiest tasks!) Every single thing she did, from making beds to feeding patients, she aimed to do as well as she could.

Still, she couldn't help wishing that Sister Stewart, her Ward Sister was easier to work for. As crusty as a loaf of bread was the best way to describe her. Already Katie had suffered the rough end of her tongue when a small boy kept refusing his cabbage. In the end Katie had dumped the cold rubbery strands in the bin. Immediately Sister descended on her like a load of cement. How dare she waste good food! How dare she deprive patients of a balanced diet! Katie's attempt to explain only made matters worse. 'How dare you answer back! I've never heard such insolence,'

Sister Stewart snapped.

Katie bit her tongue. It was a blow to be treated like that. 'Never mind. She probably treats all the student nurses that way,' she told herself later. No-one, surely, had any real complaints about her work.

She was puzzled, therefore, but not especially worried when she was told to report to Matron's Office the following Monday. All she could think of was that there might be some official form she was meant to fill out.

'Come in,' Matron's calm, measured voice responded to her knock.

'It's Nurse MacKinnon. You wanted to see me?'

'Nurse MacKinnon.' If Katie had crawled out of a drain, the grey-haired woman behind the desk couldn't have sounded less welcoming.

'You needn't sit down. I won't keep you long.'

Decidedly uneasy now, Katie tried not to fidget.

'The report on your work so far has been unfavourable,' the Matron continued coldly. 'I wish to remind you that here in the Royal Infirmary we will only permit nurses who reach our high standards to remain in training. If your work does not improve I will have no hesitation in giving you the sack. Do I make myself clear?'

'Yes, Matron,' Katie gulped.

'Very well, Nurse. You may go.'

Mechanically Katie returned to the ward. Her mind was in turmoil. How could this have happened? Her work - not of a high enough standard! But she had done everything expected of her - and more. She cared for her patients. She really did. But according to Sister Stewart, it all counted for nothing. According to Sister Stewart she was a very poor nurse.

In that moment a ball of fear and hurt seemed to lodge in Katie's heart. It was the same old story. Once she had been a bad girl, now she was a bad nurse. She could never do anything right.

Months went by. Katie finished on the children's ward and started nursing adults. She loved her work as much as ever, but her Sister-troubles continued.

Take the day the staff nurse dropped the custard, for example. There she was one moment with a huge steaming container, and the next she had skidded in under a patient's bed on her bottom and the custard was a sticky trickling mess all over the floor. But guess who got the blast of Sister's anger? The nurse under the bed? No. Katie was blamed for laughing. 'It isn't fair! Why does she always pick on me?' the girl found herself saying again and again.

There was only one other nurse who seemed to get into trouble as often as she did, and that was Jenny.

17

Jenny's mistakes were famous throughout the hospital. It was a serious act of carelessness to break a thermometer. Jenny managed to break thirty at one go by sterilizing them in boiling water. Upsetting a patient was considered an even more serious offence. Jenny managed to upset all the elderly patients on an entire ward by getting their false teeth mixed up and giving them back to the wrong owners.

Finally, one day, Jenny returned to the nurses' wing with a strange expression on her face - a mixture of guilt and relief. 'I've just come from Matron's Office,' she announced. 'It's all settled. I'm leaving.'

Leaving! The ball of fear rumbled around in Katie's stomach. So Jenny had got the sack. Who would be next? Rumble, rumble, rumble. She felt as if her whole world would come crashing about her ears if it turned out to be her.

None of this showed on her face. 'Good for you, Jenny. We'd all be a million times better off out of this dump.' She put an arm round her former room-mate's shoulder.

'Here, here,' Ann and Ishbel agreed,

Of course they had no idea of Katie's true feelings. If anyone had asked them how their madcap friend felt, they would have said she couldn't have cared less. A real dare-devil - that was the way they saw her - always planning pranks, breaking rules and giving off at the top of her voice about Sisters and Matrons.

Certainly Jenny's departure had no outward effect on Katie's behaviour. After all, she reasoned, if she was going to get into trouble anyway, she might as well enjoy herself while she was at it. And so many of the rules seemed to have been designed for no other reason than to make nurses' lives a misery. Why shouldn't she bend them?

She had a perfect opportunity for this a few months later. She was on night duty. The ward was very quiet. And she and Fiona, the other nurse on duty, were longing for a snack to keep them going till break-time.

'Right,' said Katie. 'I'm off into the kitchen to make us a pot of tea and toast.'

This was strictly against the rules. 'There'll be blue murder if the Night Sister finds out,' her companion demurred.

'She won't find out. She never does a ward-round here before eleven,' said Katie confidently.

Within minutes she was back with two cups of steaming hot tea and a plate of buttered toast. But before she had as much as lifted her cup to her lips, a shadow fell across the doorway.

'The Night Sister! She's early!' Fiona charged towards the door.

Hastily Katie shoved the tray under the low-seated armchair beside the nearest patient's bed.

'Good evening, Sister.' She did her best to appear calm and relaxed, but her heart was racing. She had really done it this time.

The Ward Round began. Patient by patient, the Sister made her way along the row of beds, every step bringing her nearer to the dreaded armchair. Oh no! Out of the corner of her eye, Katie could see wisps of steam floating up round its legs.

And then, just as it seemed Sister was bound to notice, a strange thing happened.

'Tweet...tweet...tweet...' A frantic twittering started up in the far corner of the ward.

'My goodness! That sounds like a bird,' Sister cried.

For a moment there was silence, then: 'Tweet, tweet, tweet,' the twittering sounded again.

Sister frowned and sent Fiona to investigate. 'If there's a bird trapped in the ward, we'd better get rid of it. Do you think you can capture it, Nurse?'

'I can't even see it,' Fiona called back.

The next ten minutes were spent searching for this mysterious sparrow, who miraculously (from Katie's point of view) started tweeting its head off every time the Ward Round seemed about to resume.

In the end Sister gave up. 'I'm afraid I can't stay any longer. I'll ask one of the porters to sort the thing out. Good night, everyone,' she nodded, and left.

Fiona collapsed in the armchair with a sigh of relief. What a close shave! 'I could hug that bird, wherever it is.'

'That was no bird.' Equally relieved, Katie had already worked out to whom they should really be grateful. 'It was you Dan, wasn't it?' She turned to a gypsy man recovering from an operation on his appendix. 'You saw what was about to happen and made those noises to help us. You're a real brick.'

You might have thought that after such a narrow escape, Katie would have been more careful with the rules. Not a bit of it. She carried on as usual - always a short step away from hot water.

But just as she hid from her friends how much it hurt her to be constantly in Matron's bad books, so there were other thoughts she kept hidden.

One night a middle-aged woman had been rushed into the hospital, dangerously ill. All the nurses on duty knew it was touch and go whether she would survive. And everyone was very pleased next morning to find her looking better.

'But what would have happened to her if she'd died?' Katie found herself asking. 'Where would she have gone?' The question continued to niggle at the back of her mind.

Then, a few weeks later as she travelled home to her parents (who now lived in Argyll) along the side of Loch Ness, an even more disturbing question struck her. 'What if this bus careered off the road,' she panicked. 'I could drown. What would happen to me then?'

Her enjoyment of the beautiful scenery was totally spoilt. She arrived home safely, but remained strangely uneasy for the rest of the weekend. Of course none of her family suspected she was troubled.

She had become expert at keeping such feelings to herself.

3
A FRIEND FOR LIFE

'Hello, Katie. Did you have a good weekend?' An attractive dark-haired nurse smiled warmly as Katie came back onto the ward.

'Not bad.' Katie was careful not to sound too friendly. Ever since her discovery that this particular nurse was a keen Christian, Katie had tried to have as little to do with her as possible. The last thing she wanted was a boring, religious friend.

Yet despite her intentions there was something about Jean that was hard to ignore. She wasn't as pretty as Belle or as funny as Ann, or as down-to-earth as Ishbel but she radiated some special quality that drew people to her. And now as Katie stood beside her with the questions of the weekend still buzzing about in her head - questions about life and death and heaven and God - she found herself wondering what Jean thought about these matters...

'Jean...' she began, then stopped..

'Yes?'

'It doesn't matter.' She'd changed her mind. She only half wanted to know anyway.

Anyone else might have taken offence at Katie's manner, but not Jean. She was one person who seemed to look beyond surface behaviour. In the days which followed, regardless of whether Katie welcomed her advances or not, this dark-haired girl with her kind, smiling eyes went out of her way to chat. And the more she chatted, the more envious Katie became. Here was someone happy, nice, good and not at all boring, who clearly found that faith in God made the greatest imaginable difference to life.

Were there different sorts of Christians, Katie wondered? She went to church herself most Sundays and opened her Bible from time to time. But she wasn't a Christian in the same way as Jean. Her faith didn't make her good. It didn't make her happy. And it certainly didn't stop her worrying about what would happen when she died.

Eventually she could bottle things up no longer. She picked a time when the ward wasn't particularly busy and cornered Jean in the sluice room. 'Right then. What's your idea of a proper Christian?' she demanded rather crossly to hide her concern.

Thoughtfully Jean leant back against the sterilizer. 'According to Scripture, a Christian is someone who's been born again spiritually.'

Hmmm. Katie didn't get any comfort from that. It told her what she already suspected: her church going and occasional glances at the Bible might not be enough to guarantee a place in heaven. She was a sinner; she hadn't been born again spiritually, she was pretty sure about that.

'So what happens to people who haven't been ...you know...what you said... when they die?'

Jean looked her straight in the eyes. 'The Bible teaches that only those who know Jesus as their Saviour and have his Spirit living within them will share his glory,' she replied gently.

Katie shrugged. Well, that was that. She wouldn't get in.

But her new friend wasn't prepared to give up so easily. 'I'll tell you what.' She caught Katie's arm. 'Let's get together with George this evening. He's much better at explaining things than I am.'

George was Jean's doctor boyfriend. One part of Katie's brain told her he might be worth talking to, but the other part told her it would be a total waste of time. O.K. now she knew the score. Heaven was for people like Jean - people who had some sort of special relationship with Jesus. But she could never be that sort of Christian. Why she couldn't even manage a decent relationship with Sister Stewart. So what chance did she stand with God?

Still Jean seemed so convinced that a chat with George was the answer that Katie agreed to give the meeting a try.

'Great. I'll wait for you in the corridor after work,' Jean smiled.

So it happened that at nine o'clock that evening found Katie sitting in the hospital chapel with Jean on one side and a white-coated young doctor on the other.

'This is pointless,' she informed them. 'I don't need to talk to anyone. I mean it isn't as if I've got problems.'

This didn't seem to annoy George in the slightest. 'That's fine,' he nodded. 'Jean just mentioned you wanted to know a bit more about Christianity.'

'Not really,' Katie half-rose from her seat. 'I mean, I would like to be a Christian like Jean, but I can't so there's no point in discussing it.'

'Why can't you?' His question stopped her progress towards the door.

Why couldn't she? There were so many reasons. She wasn't good. She didn't enjoy church. She had a bad temper. She disobeyed rules. And most important of all, even though she knew she was sinful she didn't want to change - at least not until she was a great deal older when she supposed she would have to sort something out for eternity.

While all these objections flooded through Katie's mind, George continued to talk, gently and persuasively, explaining that Christianity wasn't about keeping rules - it was about getting to know Jesus. He had a Bible on his knee. 'Of course what I've been telling you about God's plan of salvation is all in here.' He flipped it open as if he was about to read.

Katie told him not to bother. She was keener than ever to bring the conversation to a close. 'I already know what it says in the Bible,' she informed him. 'I read it all the time.'

'That's good. What part do you read most?'

For a moment Katie was stuck. Then in a flash of inspiration she remembered the words her mother had made her repeat all the way to Oban hospital. 'The twenty-third psalm,' she told him. That, at least, was one part of the Bible she knew like the back of her hand.

'The Lord is my shepherd,' George began to repeat the familiar verses. 'The psalmist says here the Lord is his shepherd. Can you say that, Katie?'

She looked up. Before she could answer something quite amazing occurred. It was as if the Lord Jesus himself came into the chapel. She sensed him there with them - a living shepherd, with outstretched arms, ready to lead her into eternal life. More amazing still, she knew he cared for her every bit as much as for George and Jean. The stubborn look vanished from her face. Her eyes shone. The Lord Jesus wanted to be her Lord, her Friend, her Saviour.

She whispered: 'Pray with me please, George.'

A few minutes later she was laughing, crying

and hugging Jean all at the same time. It had happened. She could feel it from the top of her head to the tip of her toes. Love. Joy. Forgiveness. 'A Christian is someone who has been born again spiritually,' Jean had said, and now that very thing had happened to her.

She fell asleep that night on top of her Bible, which had suddenly become the most exciting book in the world. When she arrived in for work next morning, no-one could help noticing the glow on her face.

'You're in good form!' Ishbel remarked.

'She must have fallen in love,' teased Ann.

Katie simply beamed. It was love that had transformed the world for her that morning - though not in the way Ann thought.

She continued to bask in that inner glow as she worked. There was the usual ward routine to get through; she had her usual share of pressures and problems; but somehow they had lost their power to upset her. Back at the nurses' home that evening she marvelled at the difference her new relationship with God had made to her day. Still, no sooner had she settled down on her bed with her Bible than she realized this wasn't the moment for reading. There was something she had to do first. Ann and Ishbel would have to be told.

Briefly the glow faded. This was going to be embarrassing. Her friends might not take her seriously. Worse still, if they did, they might not want to be friends with her anymore. Perhaps it be better to put off breaking the news for a few weeks. No - with fresh determination Katie got to her feet - she wasn't in the least ashamed of what she'd done, so why try to hide it.

Ishbel was sitting at her dressing-table when Katie charged into her room. She had just washed her hair and was combing out the tangles. 'Hi there,' she said, without turning round.

Katie didn't waste words. 'I've something to tell you, Ishbel,' she said. 'I became a Christian last night.'

The girl's reflection in the mirror assumed a look of total horror. 'How on earth did that happen?'

Katie explained. Disbelief changed to incredulity as her friend struggled to come to terms with what she was hearing. 'We're all Christians, I suppose,' she shrugged in the end.

Somehow, it seemed to Katie, she'd missed the whole point. 'That can't be right, Ishbel. I definitely wasn't a Christian before last night.'

The discussion which followed almost became an argument. A Christian, according to Ishbel, was someone who went to church and didn't do anything obviously sinful like stealing or telling lies. 'No,' Katie insisted. 'You become a Christian when you really believe that Jesus died in your place on the cross to free you from sin. It's a change that takes place in your heart.'

They left it at that. Ishbel wanted to dry her hair and Katie didn't know what else she could say. It was a bit discouraging - she had no difficulty normally talking people round to her point of view.

Fortunately telling Ann turned out to be easier than telling Ishbel.

Ann wasn't the argumentative sort. She seemed genuinely glad to see Katie so happy and said she hoped what had happened wouldn't make any difference to their friendship.

'Certainly it won't.' Katie was really relieved to hear her say that. In fairness, though, she had to warn Ann that she wouldn't be able to spend quite as much time with her as before. 'I'm going to be meeting with Jean regularly to study the Bible.'

'That's fine,' Ann smiled cheerfully. 'It's a bit like discovering a new hobby, isn't it?'

Katie smiled back. What had happened to her was far, far more important than that. A new hobby, after all, could be taken up one day and dropped the next. What she had made was the discovery of a lifetime - a Friend for Life.

One thing was certain, she had a lot to learn about getting that message across. In fact she had a lot to learn full stop.

'Don't worry about it,' Jean reassured her next

morning. 'God's Holy Spirit is living within you and you can trust him to help.'

Even as she spoke, Katie felt better. Of course it made sense. Trusting God to do things was the whole key to the Christian life. She could trust him to teach her and she could trust him to show her how to talk to her friends.

Getting down to Bible study seemed more important and more exciting than ever.

4
A SPECIAL JOB

Nobody could have been more helpful to Katie in those early days than Jean. She was always there, ready to discuss any problems without ever forcing her ideas. It was her firm belief that God himself could show Katie the things he wanted her to change about herself one step at a time.

Not everyone in the hospital shared her confidence.

A few days after the evening in the hospital chapel, Jean bumped into a group of Christian nurses in the corridor. 'We're on our way to Katie MacKinnon's room,' Rachel, the leader, explained. 'We heard she's started to call herself a Christian and we want to put her straight on a few matters.'

'You'll do no such thing.' Quiet-spoken Jean could be a force to be reckoned with when necessary.

'But Jean,' protested Rachel, 'you know what she's like. Smoking and swearing and breaking every rule in the book. She needs to be told how Christians are meant to behave.'

'God's Holy Spirit is at work in her life,' said Jean firmly. 'Changing her behaviour is his business not ours.'

'Humph!' Rachel looked as self-righteous as ever, but short of knocking Jean over, she could see there was no chance of reaching Katie's room. 'Come on, girls.' She turned on her heel. 'Katie will probably give it all up in a day or two anyway,' Jean heard her mutter as the group went back the way they had come.

The planned sermon had been rightly nipped in the bud. Before long, despite Rachel's gloomy predictions, there wasn't a single nurse in the Hospital Christian Fellowship who could have doubted Katie's commitment. Without anyone having to lecture her about anything, her life-style changed. This didn't mean she became a goody-goody. She enjoyed a joke and an outing with her friends as much as ever. But doing what God wanted clearly became her number one priority.

'It's just fantastic to know God is interested in every detail of our lives,' she exclaimed to Jean after one of their prayer-times. 'How could I ever have thought Christianity was dull.'

Many experiences lay behind these words. Day by day Katie had been discovering that God really was with her no matter what happened, and that by listening she could hear what he had to say. It was this inner voice which helped her break free from the wrong attitudes of the past.

One early lesson had begun in a very trivial way. A bottle of shampoo went missing. One minute it had been sitting by the washbasin, where she left it. The next it had vanished and Katie was left fuming helplessly, with no means of washing her hair.

Before becoming a Christian such an occurrence would have sent her charging down the corridor ready to tackle the thief if possible, and if not, to create an unholy fuss. Now she had read enough of the Bible to know this wasn't the best approach. But how would God want one of his children to behave in such circumstances? Deliberately she swallowed her fury and went back to her room.

'Lord, please show me who stole my shampoo,' she prayed.

Immediately a face flashed into her mind - the face of Evelyn - a fellow student Katie had never been able to warm to, probably because she had the annoying habit of appearing to know everything there was to know about every patient.

'Please tell me what to do?' the girl continued to pray. As clearly as before she had her answer: 'Do nothing.'

This was hard to take. Katie would much have preferred to confront Evelyn that very minute and demand the return of the shampoo. She had used the last of her meagre pay to buy it. Doing nothing would leave her shampooless for the rest of the month. She knew, though, there wasn't much point in listening to God if she wasn't prepared to obey him. He had said: 'Do nothing', so nothing was what she did. She didn't mention her suspicions to her closest friends, not even to Jean. She simply borrowed enough shampoo to tide her over until the next pay packet.

Then, just as the incident was beginning to fade from her memory, a more serious theft took place. Her newest pair of pyjamas disappeared from the pulley in the drying-room. Again Katie prayed: 'Show me the thief' - again Evelyn's face came to mind - again she asked what she should do - and this time the answer came: 'Report it.'

If obeying her first instruction had been hard, obeying this second instruction seemed even harder. After so many painful visits to Matron's Office, Katie had an instinctive mistrust of authority. Still she made herself go and report what had happened to the Home Sister. Rather to her surprise she received a sympathetic hearing. It was a serious matter indeed, the Sister agreed and promptly organized a thorough search. Within an hour the missing pyjamas had been found - in Evelyn's locker.

Katie's suspicions had been correct. All she could do was marvel when she heard the news. More than that, she could see how under God's direction she had avoided hurtful accusations and ugly scenes. She had also learnt that the authority system could work in her favour. Truly, however unattractive the path of obedience, God's method of sorting out problems was best.

Over the next three years, as Katie's spiritual growth continued, her nursing ability developed too. To her great delight she passed her final exams with flying colours and had no difficulty getting a post as a staff nurse in a hospital in Greenock. From there she went on to do a further year's training as a midwife.

Jean, meanwhile, had married George. She and Katie remained close friends and soon Katie was playing the role of adopted auntie to Jean's first baby, Alison. She was glad to see her friend so happy. It seemed clear that in marriage and bringing up a family, Jean had found God's plan for her life.

For Katie, though, the future remained unclear. Certainly she would have liked a husband and home of her own - but she hoped this wouldn't mean giving up nursing. Now that she was working with babies in the Royal Maternity Hospital, her job brought her more satisfaction than ever.

'I could happily do this for the rest of my life,' she thought to herself as she began work one Black Monday morning (Black Monday was the name given to the first Monday morning of every second month when a new group of students began training). As usual, on this particular Black Monday the Baby Unit, with its rows of perspex cots, was full of babies needing special care.

There was little Willie Miller, born weighing only two pounds, who would forget to breath every now and again and turn blue, much to everyone's concern. In the opposite cot was a lovely little West African baby whose skin colour needed to be watched too. On one occasion Katie had thought he looked paler than usual and discovered he badly needed blood. These were just two amongst many babies, some premature (like Willie), some sick - all requiring attention.

Despite her busyness, Katie was keen to meet the new students. She knew how lonely and confusing the start of a training course could be. As soon as she came off duty she made her way to the nurses' dormitory.

Sure enough there was a new student sitting on a bed.

'Hello. I'm Katie.' She approached the bed with a friendly smile, doing her best not to stare. This particular student looked so striking. She was quite young - still in her thirties - but she had mass of snow-white hair.

'Nice to meet you, Katie,' the stranger smiled back. 'My name is Jan.'

How was it that sometimes the very look in a person's eyes suggested she was a Christian? That was the way it was with Jan. Katie wasn't in the least surprised to hear that she had come to the Royal Infirmary from Bible College.

'I'm here to do my maternity training before going out to Tanzania to work as a missionary nurse,' Jan explained.

They often sat together in the canteen after that. Katie was keen to hear what Bible College was like. She had questions about missionary work too. How, for instance, was Jan going to be paid? It came as a surprise to hear that her friend was depending upon God to supply the money. This didn't sound the most reliable method - but, apparently, it worked. One morning Katie noticed a particular sparkle in Jan's eyes. She had received an anonymous gift of £200 (a large sum at that time) - just the amount she had been praying for to cover her air fare.

Katie was impressed. 'Mind you,' she observed, 'I'm very glad God isn't calling me to Bible College and missionary work, because I couldn't leave nursing.'

For a moment her friend was silent. When she looked up there was just a hint of a smile on her face. 'Don't be so sure about that,' she said quietly.

What a suggestion!

At first Katie refused to take it seriously. But as the weeks went by, no matter how hard she tried, she couldn't banish Jan's words from her thoughts.

Give up nursing and go to Bible College. She fought against the idea. 'My work is far too important to give up,' she told herself. She remembered the success stories - wonderful moments, like the day a large delivery truck had pulled up outside the Baby Unit and Willie Miller's dad had proudly taken his son home. He was a long distance lorry driver. Katie had been in stitches at the sight of such a small baby disappearing in such a huge vehicle. At the same time she had known that it was the special care unit that had kept that small baby alive.

Surely God couldn't want her to stop saving lives and go back to boring old study? It seemed such a waste. She loved her job. She was good at it. She didn't want change. But in the end she could resist the inner voice no longer. With the greatest reluctance she filled in an application form and within a matter of weeks had an interview at the Bible Training Institute in Glasgow.

The Principal, Mr. MacBeath, was a very wise man. He understood how much Katie hated the thought of studying. 'Listen, my dear. You will never regret any step you take in obedience to God,' he said kindly.

And he was right. No sooner had Katie begun her two year Bible Training course than she realized she wouldn't have missed it for worlds. It was challenging. It was fun. Above all, it was the means God had chosen to unfold his plan for her life.

Each week a missionary home on leave or representing one of the many different missionary societies would address the students.

'Serving God is like being a piece in an enormous jig-saw puzzle,' one missionary explained. 'Some pieces look the same, but they only fit into their own place. God has planned for each of us a place of our own and nobody else can fill it.'

This was an amazing thought. And one which filled Katie with the greatest excitement. Could it be that God was indeed calling her to serve him overseas? Eagerly that night she fell to her knees by her bed.

'Lord, please show me my special place,' she prayed.

5
TUG-OF-WAR

On Christmas Day almost ten years later Katie remembered that prayer. Outside her bungalow the sun blazed down on a small garden already beginning to fill up with people - tall fine-featured men, strong graceful women, beaming children - the Kipsigis people of Kenya. As a missionary with the Africa Inland Mission, Katie had been living amongst them for the last three months. A short step away from her three-bedroomed house was Litein Dispensary, a small forty-nine bed hospital and her place of work. Every morning a fresh queue of needy patients would be waiting for her attention.

In the absence of a qualified doctor, it was up to her to decide what was wrong with them and prescribe treatment. Every skill she had learned (and many she hadn't!) was being called upon daily and she was revelling in the challenge and variety.

What's more she could now understand why God had taken so long to bring her overseas. If she had come straight from Bible College to the heart of the African bush, she could never have coped with such demands. But he had seen to it that she had gained the much-needed experience first.

Her prayer had been answered. She had found her special place. What better reasons for a party!

'Chamage,' she greeted the steady stream of people all piling in over her fence. Everyone who was anyone seemed to be there - friends and their relatives and their relatives' friends. Katie would cheerfully have welcomed the whole village. She loved the Kipsigis people. With their fine features and gentle manners, she was sure that they must be one of the friendliest and most attractive peoples on earth.

Soon the party was in full swing. Plates piled high with bread and jam sandwiches were speedily cleared - their contents washed down with gallons of Coca-Cola.

Then it was time for a little exercise.

Katie produced a sisal rope.

'Have any of you ever played tug-of-war?' she asked.

Immediately she was at the centre of a circle of faces alight with curiosity and next thing a team of Kipsigis men had lined up on one side of a stick and a team of Kipsigis women on the other.

'Ready, steady, go.'

The rope went taut. Heave - heave - heave - hurrah! The contest was over almost before it had begun. A short determined effort and the women had hauled their menfolk over the stick.

Their hostesses mouth dropped open in amazement. How had this happened? Of course - suddenly she understood. In Kipsigis the women, not the men, did most of the heavy work - so they were the ones with the muscle.

Life was so different here. Briefly Katie felt removed from the laughter all around her, as if a cloud had blotted out the sun. Of course she missed her family, but that wasn't the main reason she felt sad. She was thinking of another difference: the way people here often walked over twenty miles to bring a sick child to hospital. At home in Scotland the death of a child was an unusual event. Parents there could look forward to seeing their whole family grow up. But the parents Katie met each day in the Dispensary had no such certainty. Here in Kipsigis many, many children died.

All too soon the party was over. Laughing, chattering groups of people drifted out of the garden until finally it lay silent and empty under the Kenyan night sky. Katie had just time for a bite to eat and a quick shower before returning to the Dispensary for her final ward-round of the day.

'Everything all right here, girls? Have you given out all the medicines?' she asked the two night nurses.

'Yes, Katie, we have done our work,' the older girl dutifully replied.

Her younger companion grinned and fiddled with her hair.

Katie felt a familiar prick of annoyance. This particular girl - Cheptitch was her name - had turned out to be a constant source of irritation. She was bouncy, cheerful, careless and apparently incapable of doing anything for the patients without being told. Once Katie had paid an unexpected midnight visit to the Dispensary and found her fast asleep in an empty bed.

'Just what do you think you're doing!' the newly arrived missionary had yelled. 'A patient might have taken ill and you wouldn't have known a thing about it.'

Cheptitch had hung her head. But she hadn't seemed particularly conscience-stricken. In fact it was Katie who was left feeling bad. She knew her behaviour had probably shocked the onlookers. The gentle-mannered Kipsigis never yelled.

'Good-night then.' Despite her irritation, on this occasion, she managed a smile. She had made a New Year's resolution. From now on she would handle all matters of discipline without raising her voice.

But less than a week after the party she was yelling more loudly then ever. And not just at Cheptitch this time. Somehow the teenager's carelessness seemed to have affected the entire nursing staff.

What had happened was this: a tiny baby girl weighing only two and a half pounds had been brought into the Dispensary. Her name was Chepkirui. She had been born in the Mau forest and her mother had died giving birth. Immediately Katie began to feed the child a carefully measured quantity of milk, praying that she would be able to keep it down. Then, carefully, she explained to the nurses exactly how much and how often Chepkirui was to be fed. She left the ward to hold a clinic. She returned some hours later only to find the tiny baby had been completely neglected.

Bang went her resolution! 'This is inexcusable!' she raged. 'Did I not tell you how important it was that this little one should have milk?'

'Yes, Katie,' the girls chorused.

'Did you not tell me you understood perfectly everything I was saying?'

'Yes, Katie. As for me, I understood,' they assured her one after another.

'Then why did you not do as I said?' Katie shrieked.

The girls looked at the floor and were silent. 'Katie,' one of them muttered. 'We have made you angry. We are very sorry.'

There was something odd about their behaviour. Katie began to suspect she had more to contend with here than a case of straightforward carelessness. A few more questions revealed the horrifying truth. The girls neglect of Chepkirui had been deliberate. In their eyes if God intended babies to live, he made sure they were born at the right time. Chepkirui had been born too early; therefore she was not meant to survive.

'But that simply isn't true,' Katie protested. 'God loves every baby, no matter how small. It is for this very reason he has placed Chepkirui in our care.'

She sensed, though, that her thoughts were as foreign as her language. The girls would continue to view Chepkirui in the traditional way.

In the days which followed her ward-problems got worse. Another baby, a little boy this time, came into the Dispensary. His name was Kipngeno. His mother had given birth normally in another hospital, then died shortly afterwards. Now at the age of three months, Kipngeno was very sick. He would feed hungrily and appear satisfied; then suddenly his mouth would twist to an impossible angle up the side of his face, his eyes would become huge and staring, and he would vomit up the entire contents of his stomach. Often, after such an attack, he would run a high fever. Katie had never come across a case like it. She knew that if Kipngeno lost more weight he would certainly die.

If the girls had seen little point in caring for Chepkirui, they saw no point whatsoever in looking after Kipngeno. 'That baby was cursed by the witch-doctors,' they told Katie. 'There's no hope for him.'

Cursed by witchdoctors? A baby? Katie had never heard of such a thing. The idea so disturbed her she drove all the way to the hospital where Kipnegno had been born to consult the doctor.

Some hours later she returned along the dirt track in a complete state of shock. The doctor - a European - had agreed with the girls. 'Over the years I've been forced to take this cursing business seriously,' he had sighed. 'In all likelihood the baby will die.'

What was to be done? Obviously if what the doctor said was true no ordinary medicine would help Kipngeno.

That evening Katie got together with two or three other missionaries and did the only thing they could. They prayed - asking God to break the hold of evil on Kipnegno's life and make him better.

And that night, for the first time, Kipnegno happily took his ten o'clock feed. All his unnatural symptoms - the twisted mouth, glazed eyes and sudden fevers - had disappeared.

'God has healed Kipngeno! He's keeping his food down,' Katie joyfully announced to the other nurses next morning.

Oh dear! One look at their doubtful faces told

her she was wasting her breath. It would take a lot more than this to convince them that babies such as Kipngeno could live.

From feeling on top of the world Katie was plummeted into new depths of confusion. It was like being caught in a real-life game of tug-of-war. She felt torn between wanting the very best for Kipngeno and Chepkirui and not wanting to be constantly yelling at the nursing staff.

One thing was certain. She needed to spend as much time as possible supervising in the Dispensary. The fortnight's holiday she had planned for the month of January was now out of the question.

Or was it? Something happened a few days later which brought matters to a head. Katie walked into the ward and found Cheptitch lounging up against a wall. A few feet away lay a sick child with a jug of Ribena mixed with sugar and salt beside her bed. In order to stay alive the young patient needed to be given regular sips of the mixture throughout the day. But this particular jug was full to the brim.

Something went snap in Katie's mind. At any time such carelessness would have made her angry, but after all that had happened it sent her into a total rage. 'Cheptitch, you haven't given that child a single sip to drink all morning,' she yelled. 'Just pack your box and go. You're fired!'

Afterwards she felt ashamed. She did not regret her decision, for Cheptitch would never have made a good nurse. But she regretted the way she had lost her temper. The way she had yelled. Being tired made it so much harder to be patient.

I really do need a break from the Dispensary, she thought - two weeks of reading, eating and sleeping under my own roof.

But how could she leave Kipngeno and Chepkirui? No sooner had she asked the question than the perfect answer flashed into her mind. Of course! Why hadn't she thought of it sooner! Kipngeno and Chepkirui could come too.

6
KIPKOECH

Katie's missionary friends thought she was mad. 'A fortnight spent looking after two babies! What sort of holiday is that!'

'My sort of holiday.' Katie paused just long enough to reply. She was checking down the list of things she would need: two cots, cot sheets, nappies, a supply of lactogen milk...

Within less than twenty-four hours Kipngeno and Chepkirui had been transferred to her bungalow. And just as Katie had expected, their presence transformed the next fortnight into the holiday of a lifetime. At last she had freedom to do everything she possibly could to bring them back to health, cuddling them, praying for them, even talking to them; anything to let them know they really mattered, not just to her, but to God.

All too soon it was time to go back to work. Katie stood by the babies' cots, watching them as they slept. Love, indeed, had worked wonders. They had been such scrawny, pathetic, little scraps when they arrived. Now their cheeks had filled out and they looked the picture of contentment.

But who would love them when they went back to the Dispensary? No-one - that was the painful answer. The nurses just wouldn't be able to see their way to loving a premature baby, or one that had been cursed. And without love they could so easily lose ground.

'I'd be the most foolish nurse in Kenya if I let that happen,' Katie said to herself as she climbed into bed. 'I'll keep them here for another two weeks.'

Two months later Kipngeno and Chepkirui were still with her - chubby, bright-eyed and full of mischief. Somehow the right time for moving them back to the Dispensary had never come. Instead Katie had developed a new routine: she was up every morning at 4:45 a.m. to feed the babies, read her Bible and pray. At 6:00 a.m. she would put them into their day clothes, give them their porridge and do all the washing. At 7:30 she would have her own breakfast before going down to the Dispensary to begin work!

And so it went on. A nurse would stay in the house with the children for the periods when Katie had to be away. But in between clinics and ward rounds, Katie was able to nip back to make sure that Kipngeno and Chepkirui got all the love they needed to help them grow strong.

The main problem, though, remained unsolved. Kipngeno and Chepkirui might be well on their way to good health, but the people of the area still believed that premature babies were not meant to live, and that children who had been cursed would definitely die. It wasn't that they were uncaring, or that they didn't want such children to survive, it was just that they had never known anything different.

'If only there was something I could do to help them understand.' Katie racked her brain to think of a method. Shouting definitely didn't work; neither did her attempts to explain quietly. It seemed she had no choice but to accept things the way they were. So did this mean that hundreds of babies like Kipngeno and Chepkirui would still have no-one to fight for their lives?

What a horrible thought! The tug-of-war went on more furiously than ever in Katie's heart. At times she almost felt it would tear her apart.

'Lord, please help me. Please show me what to do about this,' she prayed.

God had an answer. He had planned it and set it in motion months before Katie had even uttered her prayer. But Katie suspected nothing of this: from her point of view the weeks slipped by, Kipngeno and Chepkirui got bigger and stronger - they had even started to pull themselves up in their cots - and still she could see no way out of her problem.

Then - suddenly - the breakthrough!

The day started off in a perfectly ordinary way.

Katie got up at the usual time, did all the usual things, and was in the middle of washing her hair before going over to the Dispensary when there was a knock at her door.

'I am here to tell you to come to the Dispensary.' A nurse stood on the doorstep looking important.

With a sigh, Katie wrapped a towel round her head. 'What's the matter?' she asked.

At this the girl looked more pleased with herself than ever. 'There is a woman in the ward with a small, small baby.'

A premature baby. 'Stay here with the children.' Katie was on her feet in an instant and out through the door.

Breathless, she reached the maternity ward to find a woman on a bed with a baby-shaped bundle by her side.

'Chamage,' Katie greeted her. ' I have come to see your baby.'

'Achamage,' the woman responded. But she didn't display any of the usual enthusiasm to show off her child.

'I have heard your baby is very small and in need of special care,' Katie prompted.

The woman gazed back bleakly. 'You are wrong. It is not a baby. It is a monkey.'

A monkey! Katie could hardly believe her ears. Perhaps she had misunderstood. Gently she pulled back the cloth round the mysterious bundle to reveal the red wrinkled face of - yes definitely - a tiny baby.

'It is a monkey,' the woman insisted, staring into space.

More clearly than ever Katie saw the tragedy of the situation. This woman wanted to love her child, but couldn't let herself. She was calling it a monkey (it turned out that this was the local term for all premature babies) because she knew it was too small to live.

'Please let me look after your baby for you,' she pleaded.

'No,' the woman now picked up the bundle and clasped it firmly. 'You will only grow fond of it and it will die and then you will be sorry.'

The missionary held out her arms. 'Perhaps if I look after it, it will live and then we will both be glad.'

'It is a monkey,' the woman muttered. But there was a flicker of hope in her eyes. Dare she trust this white woman? Was it safe to do as she asked? For a long moment hope battled against doubt. At last she made up her mind. 'Here. Take it!'

'Thank you, Lord,' Katie whispered delightedly as she carried the precious bundle to the house.

But back in her living-room, her joy quickly

faded. The baby was even smaller than she had expected - the sort of size Willie Miller had been when he arrived in the Special Baby Unit. Like Willie this baby was too small to feed and might stop breathing at any moment. At home in Scotland he would have been put straight into an incubator, but there was no such medical equipment here to help him survive.

Have I raised his mother's hopes simply to dash them to pieces? Katie wondered, cradling the baby in her arms. She hardly knew where to put such a mite. He would be lost in a cot.

Such was her anxiety that it was a moment or two before she noticed the commotion going on outside. The sound of a truck...raised voices...someone shouting instructions over her garden gate...

She reached the window just in time to see a very large crate being dumped over the fence.

'Hey there,' she shot out of the house. 'Just put that crate back on your lorry and take it away.'

The truck driver grinned and scratched his head.

'Are you Miss Katie MacKinnon?'

'Yes.'

'Then this crate's for you.'

'But I haven't ordered anything!' Katie glared resentfully at the huge wooden box. On another occasion she might have enjoyed the mystery of it all, but at that moment all she could think of was the tiny baby lying on her living-room settee. Still there was only one thing for it - she would have to find out what was inside.

'Come on. Let's get it open.' The words brought a dozen delighted spectators scrambling over the fence to help. Eagerly they surrounded the crate, pushing and prising. Then came the sound of splintering wood as one of the boards was raised.

'It looks like a glass box,' called James, the Dispensary handy-man.

What! Katie elbowed him aside to look for herself. Sure enough beneath the wooden boards she could see a smooth glass surface.

She gasped, scarcely able to believe her senses. If what she was seeing was true this was indeed one of the most wonderful, incredible experiences of her life. 'Quick, quick. Get it out. But please be very careful!' The packaging was removed and, yes, there it was, the one thing that could save the life of the baby on the settee. A gleaming chrome-framed incubator, complete with plug was now standing right outside her front door.

It wasn't until some time later that she learnt the history of the miracle. A hospital in the United States had been modernizing their Baby Unit.

Sally, a missionary nurse, who had worked in the Dispensary had asked that some of the older equipment should be sent to Litein. The hospital authorities had agreed, packed up an incubator and shipped it out.

Of course no-one had any idea how long the delivery would take - six months? eight months? a year? There was a possibility that it might never arrive, and, even if it did, that it might be damaged beyond repair. But God had over-ruled, making sure that the incubator arrived in perfect working order at exactly the moment it was needed most.

'God sent this piece of equipment specially to save the life of your little son,' Katie was able to tell the baby's mother that afternoon.

The woman's eyes were huge. There was her baby - Kipkoech, she had now named him - lying with no clothes on in a glass box! She made her way straight back to the Dispensary to spread the amazing news amongst her friends.

Within the hour there was a queue of maternity patients on Katie's doorstep. Everyone wanted to see Kipkoech and hear his story for themselves. Word spread to the villages, and soon there were so many visitors to the house, all wanting to hear what God had done, that the Dispensary Evangelist took charge.

With a thankful heart Katie heard him sharing the good news of the Gospel with the people, explaining as he did so, that no-one, not even the smallest child, was beyond the reach of God's love.

The people listened carefully to every word. Eventually Kipkoech's mother beckoned Katie aside.

'Me, I have learned something very important,' she whispered.

'And what is that?' Katie asked.

The woman beamed and pointed at the incubator. 'There are no monkeys. There are only babies.'

No monkeys. Only babies. The missionary felt like jumping for joy. At last the message was getting through. For the first time people were recognizing that with special care the smallest and weakest children in their villages could have a future. God had found the perfect way of showing them - the way she had searched for in vain. He had used a tiny baby in an incubator.

Of course Kipkoech didn't remain in the incubator. Within a short time he was strong enough to sleep in an ordinary cot and his place had been taken by another premature baby - Kipkirui. At around the same time a little girl badly in need of nursing care was brought to Katie's home. Her name was Chebet.

Kipngeno, Chepkirui, Kipkoech, Kipkirui and Chebet. That meant Katie had a family of five in her spare rooms; five sets of nappies to be washed, five tummies to be filled, five bodies to be dressed, five faces to be wiped - and she was still working full-time in the Dispensary.

7

A FRIEND IN NEED

'You'll never be able to manage.'

Katie's visitor had come with one purpose in mind - to tell her missionary colleague that she should stop trying to do two jobs at once. For a solid ten minutes she had been sitting there, a large Bible open on her lap. 'You were sent here to work in a Dispensary,' she lectured. 'If God had meant you to have children in your home he would have given you a husband and let you have them in the normal way. And anyway, you can't afford it. Have you thought where the money's going to come from to feed five children as well as yourself?

Katie gritted her teeth. She was close to losing her temper. At the same time she knew her friend had come because she cared.

'All I can say is that I truly believe that God brought these five children into my home.' She gave a sudden smile. 'So I'm trusting him to provide for them.'

'And if he doesn't?'

'He has up until now.'

'Humph.' Still far from satisfied, Ellen rose to her feet.

'You're making a huge mistake,' she called from the door. She had gone. With a sigh of relief, Katie went into the kitchen and put on the kettle. She felt urgently in need of a cup of coffee.

She thought about what Ellen had said as she sipped. From the human point of view she had to admit her friend's arguments made sense. It was hard to see how she could continue to feed five growing children on a single missionary allowance. Somehow she had made ends meet so far. There was food in the cupboard. She didn't have any debts. But managing would be more difficult in the months ahead: the children would be bigger, everything would cost more. 'I suppose I ought to be worried,' Katie thought, as she drained her cup. Surprisingly, she wasn't. Instead she had a deep inner peace. Over the years she had learnt to recognize this as a sign that the Holy Spirit was at work.

Something happened a short time later which made her more certain of this than ever.

It was the last week in the month - the time her monthly cheque usually arrived. 'I'm off to the Post Office,' Katie told the nurses at the Dispensary. Since there was no such thing as a postal delivery service in Litein, she had to collect her own mail.

The Post Office was a strange-looking building with one wall made up entirely of row upon row of Post Office boxes, each with its own number, lock and key. Eagerly Katie unlocked her box and looked inside. Great! There was the envelope she had been expecting - long, white, and rectangular with the Mission post mark in one corner.

But what was this! A glance at the cheque inside revealed that it was made out for more than usual. Several pounds more. For the first time ever someone had sent in an extra gift.

'How nice!' Katie thought as she made her way to the car.

Unfortunately this nice surprise was followed by rather a nasty one. The following morning Kipkirui wasn't his usual happy self. He didn't eat his porridge, nor did he want to play. Katie decided to keep a close eye on him in case he was sickening for something.

At lunch-time the little boy was certainly no better. His eyes looked heavy and he seemed a little breathless. During the afternoon this breathlessness got worse until by tea-time Katie knew she could not delay a moment longer. She wrapped the sick child in a blanket, bundled him into the car and set off for the nearest hospital.

There Kipkirui was examined by a doctor. He had a nasty chest infection, it turned out. 'Start him on this medicine straight away.' The doctor wrote out a prescription. 'And bring him back next week.'

Suddenly Katie felt embarrassed. She had left in such a hurry she hadn't brought any money to pay.

'Don't worry.' Kindly the doctor patted Kipkirui's curly head. 'You can settle up later.'

Kipkirui recovered quickly. His chest was almost clear on his second hospital visit. This time Katie had come prepared with a purseful of Kenyan shillings.

'Goodness!' she gasped when she saw the bill.

'Is something wrong?' asked the doctor.

'No, nothing, it's just such a coincidence!'

The bill for Kipkirui's treatment added up to exactly the same amount as the gift she had received.

From that time on Katie saw God's provision for the children again and again. The cheques she collected at the Post Office never failed to contain extra gifts. It wasn't that the people at home had heard she needed more money. (She had been so busy, she hadn't had time to write.) But every month those gifts came flowing in - sometimes more, sometimes less - but always just enough to cover the children's needs.

What a pity I can't collect extra energy in the same way, she thought one evening. The day had been particularly hectic. More than anything else she longed for a full night's sleep - something quite out of the question with so many babies in the house. Her legs felt like lead as she dragged herself into the kitchen to make up bottles for the ten o'clock feeds. It was one of the rare occasions when she found herself wondering where she would find the strength to keep going.

It seemed the last straw when a car pulled up outside her house.

'Oh no!' she thought. Normally she loved visitors, but not this evening - not when she was so tired. Her face brightened slightly when she saw who her callers were. Eric and Emily Barnett - two older missionaries with a great deal of wisdom and experience.

But why on earth were they here? Astonished, Katie watched them unpack a very odd assortment of stuff from their car-boot.

Ten seconds later all was explained. 'There's no need to do anything,' announced Emily, as Eric struggled through the door with a sleeping-bag under each arm. 'Just go off to your bed. We'll take care of the children.'

Next morning, after the best sleep ever, Katie arrived into the living-room to find her helpers side by side on the settee each with a baby and a feeding-bottle in hand.

'I don't know how to thank you.' She felt like hugging them both.

'It was nothing.' Business-like as ever, Emily winded the child on her knee.

But she was wrong. That little break had meant more than Katie could ever say. Not only had it cured her tiredness, it had come as yet another sign of God's love, another sign that having the children in her home was part of his plan.

And then, as suddenly as it had started, the provision stopped.

One day Katie went to the Post Office to discover that her allowance was back to its usual size. Within a couple of weeks she was broke. A few days later there was hardly a scrap of food left in the larder.

What's going to happen now? she wondered anxiously as she used the last of her millet to make porridge for breakfast.

Comforting herself with the thought that God wouldn't let the children go hungry, she went over to the Dispensary to begin work.

'Would you check my Post Office Box?' she asked James, the Dispensary handyman. Surely today's mail would bring an answer to her problem.

But it didn't. James returned from his errand with nothing but a smile.

I'll look in the kitchen. Perhaps the cupboards aren't empty after all. Perhaps I've missed something. Katie tried to keep up her spirits as she returned home for a mid-morning cup of coffee. Again her hopes were disappointed. All she found was emptiness: no flour, no rice, no maize, no beans, no nothing.

The minutes ticked past, each bringing her closer to the hour the children were due to be fed. It was terrible to think that she had no way to satisfy their hunger. Faith battled with doubt at the sight of the bare shelves. Why was this happening?

'God must be telling me something,' Katie told herself firmly. But what?

She was still puzzling over this when Dorcas, the nurse on duty in the house, knocked on the door.

'We are having visitors,' she announced.

Sure enough Katie found a group of graceful Kipsigis women from the nearby village of Rungut seated in her living-room.

'We bring gifts for you and the children,' the leader said shyly.

Only then did Katie notice the miracle on her living-room table. Why how wonderful! She could hardly believe her eyes. It was piled high with food - millet, eggs, milk, pineapples - easily enough to see her through to the end of the month.

But what the ladies had to say was more thrilling still.

They had come with words of encouragement. The church in Rungut recognized the great value of her work, they explained. Up until now there had been nowhere for children to go if their parents died and their relatives couldn't afford to take them in. 'Now through this house God is providing a home for such children,' the leader exclaimed. 'The work you are doing is very important work. We, in the Rungut church, are praying that God will bless it and make it grow.'

Grow!! The word continued to echo in Katie's brain long after her visitors had left. Had God allowed the crisis in her larder in order to tell her this? From the human point of view it didn't make sense. How could her work grow? Five children were already pushing her resources to the limit.

Katie didn't have any answers. What she did have was faith. Softly insistent above the voice of common sense she heard the voice of the Spirit: 'All things are possible with God.'

8

STRONGER THAN SATAN

Things couldn't have worked out better. Within a few short years the work which had begun with two tiny babies in the spare room of a missionary bungalow had developed into an Official Children's Centre catering for needy children from all over the area. Each step of the way, as numbers had grown (from five children to six, from six to fourteen, from fourteen to twenty-two). God had made the impossible possible.

Mrs. Rookmaaker, the Secretary of a Dutch organisation committed to saving the lives of children, had paid Katie a visit. 'From now on we will send you money for food every month,' she promised.

Betty, Faith and Diana, volunteers with a youth organisation called Campus Crusade, came to Litein and proved very capable of looking after the Dispensary.

Finally Matthew and Priscilla - a very special couple indeed - clearly heard God's call to them to work with children. So when Mrs. Rookmaaker offered to pay for an African Manager and his wife to help Katie run the Children's Centre, there they were ready for action - the ideal people for the job.

What Katie liked best about this new arrangement was the sense of being part of a team. At long last the demands of each day were fitting comfortably into twenty-four hours. The Children's Centre now occupied two houses. Matthew and Priscilla lived in the biggest one with most of the children (some were orphans for whom it was their permanent home; others would return to their villages after a few months), while she lived in the smaller house, with the children who needed special care. Of the five original children only Kipngeno and Chebet remained. Chepkirui, Kipkirui and Kipkoech had gone back to their families.

They would always hold a special place in Katie's heart. Kipkoech's homecoming, in particular, had been an unforgettable experience. An enormous gathering of people from all the surrounding villages had been waiting outside his parents' home to greet the little boy. The Dispensary Evangelist told them what the Bible taught about the importance of caring for children, and warned that it was the responsibility of the whole village to see that Kipkoech was not neglected in any way. He also pointed out that the same loving God who had supplied an incubator to keep this child alive wanted people everywhere to live eternally through faith in Jesus Christ. To Katie's joy, many had openly put their trust in the Lord that day.

But there was a dark side to this spiritual openness. Yes, people were open to the power of the Gospel, but they were equally open to the spiritual influences bound up with superstition, witch-doctors and idol worship.

After her early experience with Kipngeno, Katie knew these things were no joke. The little boy had grown up into the cutest youngster who ever toddled about on two sturdy legs. Yet his father didn't seem to want to have him home. Deep down, Katie suspected, the man was still afraid that the curse which had once threatened his little son's life might still be active, that Kipngeno might somehow bring him bad luck. This was nonsense. At the same time she could see for herself that the power of the witch-doctors was a very real force.

'When it comes to coping with curses what are missionaries meant to do?' she wondered from time to time. She felt she had an important lesson or two to learn in this area. But it wasn't until a few months after Matthew and Priscilla had joined her in the work, that the matter became urgent.

It was ten o'clock in the evening. Katie sat in her living-room enjoying the unusual peace and quiet. She always welcomed this stage of the day. Any moment now Matthew and Priscilla would arrive to chat over a bedtime drink. They would share all the different things that had happened and pray for each of the children by name.

Katie sighed. Normally she was more than happy to do her fair share of the talking. Tonight, though, she didn't feel in a talkative mood. She had had such a strange experience that day. The more she thought of it the stranger it seemed - one of the children had walked up a wall.

'You mean, she climbed a wall,' Matthew would undoubtedly smile.

But Chebet had not climbed. She had walked - horizontally, as if for a few brief seconds the force of gravity had mysteriously altered and her body had become as weightless as a fly. 'Chebet!' Katie had screamed and immediately snatched the child down, praying urgently that she would come to no harm.

It had been over so fast and now seemed like a bad dream. Katie sighed again. She was beginning to doubt her senses; why, the very idea of Chebet being weightless seemed laughable. Chebet - the chubbiest baby in the house! The missionary decided to put the whole disturbing incident out of her mind.

Still over the next few weeks she found herself keeping a closer eye than usual on the little girl. Chebet, for her part, kept both feet firmly on the ground. She played happily, slept soundly, ate well. In other words she appeared as healthy and normal as ever a child could be.

It came as something of a puzzle when an elderly woman came to the Home and asked if Chebet was still alive.

'Of course she's alive. She's never been sick,' said Katie cheerfully.

The woman nodded. 'Then may I see her?'

Katie could see no reason to refuse the request. Relatives often came to see the children. In fact she seemed to remember that this woman, with her wrinkled face and keen dark eyes, had visited Chebet once before.

'Certainly. She's over there.' The missionary pointed to the children's play area.

With her usual beaming smile Chebet ran to meet them. The woman knelt down, took her in her arms and rocked her, crooning into her ear. Katie couldn't understand the words. She assumed the woman was murmuring something in her tribal language - a lullaby perhaps. The crooning went on for several minutes and then the woman left.

The rest of the afternoon passed quickly. Between attending to the children and buzzing backwards and forwards to the wards, Katie had plenty to keep her busy. (Betty and Sylvia were doing a great job in the Dispensary but they didn't have the knowledge or experience needed to deal with difficult cases.) In the early evening another visitor arrived - an African pastor, this time. Katie and Matthew had just sat down to chat to him when the door burst open and Priscilla ran into the room.

'There is a problem! Chebet has a fever!' she cried.

One look at the child in her arms and Katie could see the reason for her alarm. Chebet's eyes were glazed and her forehead was burning hot. Then, in front of their eyes, it happened - the same incredible stunt as before. The little girl broke free from Priscilla's grasp, toddled across to the wall and next thing she was standing on it, in mid-air, three feet from the ground.

For the second time in as many months Katie snatched the child down. As she did so, she remembered something else that had happened twice - the old woman's visit. Yes, it had been after her first appearance that the first wall-walking incident had taken place. And now this. The missionary shivered. Suddenly she felt sure that the woman, whoever she was, had returned with nothing but evil in mind. Her crooning had been no lullaby, but a curse.

Several days passed. The memory of the incident hung like a shadow at the back of Katie's mind. Finally she decided to consult Pastor Philip - the chairman of the Dispensary Management Committee.

'I'm just not prepared for this sort of thing. I don't know how to handle it,' she thought as she jolted along the dirt track as fast as she dared towards his home. She hoped Pastor Philip would be able to throw some light on the matter. Her main fear was that she might have difficulty convincing him that the story was true.

It sounded more incredible than ever in the airy quiet of the pastor's house. But to Katie's surprise the elderly man calmly accepted every word.

'So, then, why have you come?' he inquired in the end.

Why had she come? Katie thought that was obvious. 'Because the child walked up the wall!'

'Has she suffered any bad effects?'

'No.' This indeed was something to be thankful for. 'As soon as we realized what was happening - that there was some sort of evil at work - we prayed in the name of Jesus - and since then Chebet's been fine.'

'So why have you come?'

The same question again. This time the missionary gave a totally honest answer.

'Because...because I'm scared, that's why.'

'Ah.' Pastor Philip smiled slightly, as if he had suspected as much all along. He opened the Bible on his desk. 'You know, Katie, many people in my country look for spiritual help in the wrong places; they turn to the witch-doctors or to figures made of wood which they call gods. '

Katie nodded. She was mentally adding some of the things people turned to at home: horoscopes, tarot cards, mediums, ouija boards...

'They do not know the Word of God,' Pastor Philip continued. 'They do not understand that it is the devil himself who responds to their seekings, that his purpose is not to help but to destroy.'

'But listen.' Here he raised one finger for emphasis, pausing and looking her directly in the eyes. 'Christians need not fear such evil. We can pray, as you did, in the Name of Jesus and know that the power of his Spirit is the strongest power of all.'

It sounded so simple when put like that. And clearly, as far as Pastor Philip was concerned, there was nothing more to be said.

Sooner than she expected Katie was driving back the way she had come. She passed a row of colourful wooden stalls with people selling their wares. She watched a team of oxen ploughing against a gentle background of undulating hills. And gradually, as she looked, the pastor's words took root in her heart. She drank in their wonderful truth: this country and all the people in it belonged to the Lord. Oh yes, the devil might have a certain limited control over some people's hearts and minds. But nothing could stand in the way of the Gospel. No potion. No idol. No curse. In the distance she saw sunlight glinting off the windows of the Children's Centre. 'Nothing can happen within those walls that God can't handle,' she found herself thinking.

Her fear, she suddenly realized, had gone.

9

NO SUPPER FOR SAMMY

'Good morning, Miss MacKinnon.' The tall Englishman held out his hand. 'My colleagues and I have been intending to pay you a visit for some time. We're from the Ministry of Health.'

The Ministry of Health! Katie felt nervous flutters in her stomach. 'Do come in.' She tried to make the invitation sound as warm as possible, hoping desperately that there hadn't been complaints about the Home.

She needn't have worried. Her unexpected visitors turned out to be friendlier than they looked. They certainly hadn't come to investigate complaints - quite the opposite in fact. They had come because reports about the Children's Centre had been so good. 'The death-rate here seems to be lower than anywhere else,' they explained. 'Are you sure that there hasn't been some mistake in the figures?'

No mistake at all, Katie beamed. And to prove the point she spent the next half an hour introducing them to some of the children. There was Chebet of course; and Chepkirui, another little girl, whose father was now serving a prison sentence for beating her mother to death. For a long time afterwards any sound resembling someone being beaten had made Chepkirui vomit, but now, after much prayer, she was able to greet the visitors with a smile.

Next in the line were twin boys, Frank and Henry. 'Frank had the most dreadful squint when he arrived,' Katie explained. 'Luckily we have a wonderful eye specialist - Dr. Mike Absolom - who gives up part of his holidays every second year to do operations here and in Uganda.'

'He certainly did a good job there,' one of the doctors murmured, as Frank, with bright-eyed directness, met his gaze. The little boy beamed, but before he could make any further progress towards the visitor's knee, sturdy little Sammy had elbowed him out of the limelight.

Sammy, of course, was still too young to talk to the visitors himself; but he had a remarkable story to tell.

His mother had travelled a long distance to bring him to the Children's Centre. Her distress as she stood on Katie's doorstep had been plain to see. Sammy was ten months old at the time, but he had weighed only five pounds.

'He is too sick to grow,' the woman explained. 'Every time I feed him he vomits.'

'Well, we'll see what we can do for him here.' Katie felt her spirit rise to the challenge. 'With God's help one of these days your little Sammy will be toddling around with all the rest of the children.'

The woman's eyes lit up. 'With God's help,' she nodded, placing her son in the Katie's arms.

As soon as the woman left, Katie made up a feed of milk in a sterilised bottle. 'Right, let's find out how much of this stays down!' She gave it to Sammy carefully, holding the bottle at just the right angle to make sure there was no air in the teat.

What a waste of time! Within moments of finishing the baby had brought the whole thing back up.

'No wonder he hasn't grown when his stomach keeps behaving like that,' the missionary thought.

Suddenly she had a brain-wave. She put Sammy into his cot and charged off to the kitchen. For several moments she rummaged through the store-cupboard, through sacks and bags and boxes of all sizes and descriptions until at last she found the carton she was looking for.

Ten minutes later she was feeding Sammy again - this time with a mixture of soya bean extract. And this time the little boy's stomach behaved itself perfectly. Sammy wasn't sick. He simply shut his eyes and went to sleep, just like a baby should after a good dinner!

'Well, my little fellow,' smiled Katie triumphantly. 'I think we've got to the root of your problem.'

Sammy, she was now almost certain, was allergic to ordinary milk.

And so it turned out. After a mere six weeks on his soya milk diet Sammy was a different boy: he was putting on weight, sitting up, smiling. But another problem loomed ahead.

What would happen when the carton of soya bean extract ran done? None of the shops locally kept such a specialized product in stock.

'I'll have to go to Kericho to get the stuff,' Katie told Matthew.

But it wasn't that simple.

In the heat of the afternoon one very frustrated missionary knocked on the door of the Famine Relief Agency.

Marilyn, the administrator, immediately knew that something was wrong. 'Hello, Katie. What can we do for you? You look worried.'

'I am worried.' Wearily Katie leant against the wall. 'We've a food problem in the Children's Centre. I need to get hold of some soya milk powder fast.

'Soya milk powder? Sorry, we can't help there. Wouldn't ordinary milk powder do instead?'

'No.' Katie's anxious frown deepened as she explained about Sammy. 'I've spent the whole afternoon driving around. Your agency was my last hope.'

How Marilyn wished she could help! But there

was famine in the area. Even basic foodstuffs were scarce, and soya bean extract was difficult to get at the best of times.

Katie returned from her shopping trip empty-handed.

'There's only enough powder left for two more feeds - Sammy's breakfast and dinner tomorrow,' she thought with a pang.

Usually it was late evening when the Children's Centre team got together to pray for the children's needs. Today though, Katie was so concerned about what would happen if Sammy had to go back to ordinary milk, she slipped away into her own room.

There she knelt by her bed. Of course she had prayed about the problem before, but never quite as earnestly as this.

'Dear Father, I know you are with me in this work and that you love Sammy very much. Please, please show me where I can find food for him.'

The words were no sooner out of her mouth than the telephone rang. Marilyn's voice sounded faint but clear at the end of the line. 'We've just had a message from Mombasa. A plane full of supplies is due to land on Kericho airstrip in an hour's time.'

Katie was out of her house like a bullet, and into her car. Jolting her way back towards Kericho, she felt a growing sense of expectation. Of course she had no reason to believe that there would be a carton of soya bean extract on board that plane. When people were sending supplies they usually majored on things like flour, medicines and blankets. The timing of the phone-call, though, seemed so promising.

She reached the airstrip with minutes to spare, in time to watch the small two-seater land. The pilot jumped from the cockpit.

'Looking for food?' he greeted Katie cheerfully.

Katie's heart pounded as she made her request. 'All I want is a carton of soya milk powder. Have you got one?'

'Nope,' the pilot shook his head.

'Oh,' Katie gasped in disappointment. And then she saw the twinkle in his eyes.

'Like I said, I haven't got one; I've got thirty-two cartons of the stuff on board!'

'That's enough powder to keep Sammy going until he's ready for school!' Katie told Marilyn excitedly next morning. 'It just goes to show: God's ways of doing things are so much bigger and better than ours.'

Behind her, in the kitchen, was a store-cupboard jam-packed with soya bean extract. And in her heart she had stored up yet another experience of God's faithfulness - another example of the wonderful things that could happen with a Divine

Manager in charge of the Home.

The whole set-up clearly made a big impression on the visiting officials. There they were surrounded by angelically smiling children, many of whom, according to the medical text-books, should never have survived.

'You mean to tell us that some of these kids had lost over twenty-five percent of the skin from their bodies!' The senior doctor scratched his head.

'That's right,' Katie nodded. She knew exactly what he was thinking. Severe malnutrition (or lack of proper food) caused skin loss, and, according to the text-books, where over twenty-five percent of a child's skin was affected, the chances of recovery were slim. So how could so many of these beaming bright-eyed children have beaten the odds? With an inward smile she heard the doctor inquire about her methods of treatment. No doubt he hoped to learn of some new revolutionary diet that could be introduced more widely and written up in medical journals. Well, he was in for a shock.

She looked at Sammy. Soon he would return home, accompanied by his delighted mother and half-a-dozen other relatives all carrying cartons of soya milk! His story was a perfect illustration of the principles along which the Children's Centre ran.

'Practical care plus prayer,' she stated simply. 'Matthew, Priscilla and I pray for our sick children every night. Often the children get better. Sometimes, to our great grief, they do not. But whatever the outcome we know we are praying to a loving Father who wants the best for every child. That, we believe, is the secret of our success.'

10
A FRIEND IN DANGER

It was Sunday morning. Sunday mornings were never too peaceful in the Children's Centre, but this one was even less peaceful than usual. Katie woke up to the sound of a furious banging and hammering. Staring out of her window, she saw that a set of scaffolding had been erected directly opposite her home. 'Don't those workmen know this is supposed to be a day of rest!' she thought grimly.

Either they did know and didn't care, or else the job they were doing was so urgent it couldn't wait. For whatever reason, the hammering continued right through breakfast and was still going strong as Katie changed into her cool Sunday dress with its broad white collar.

She looked at her watch and picked up her car keys. Time for church. Bang, bang, bang, bang. The noise sounded louder than ever when she opened the door.

She stepped outside. Well, one good thing could be said for those builders - they were certainly friendly. First one man pointed down at her and waved. Then the man beside him waved too. And suddenly they were all at it - every workman on the building was waving and shouting down at her!

'Good morning to you too,' Katie waved back.

This reaction clearly wasn't enough to satisfy her admirers. With a bloodchilling yell the foreman slithered down to the ground and shot across the road. Katie had only time to wonder if he had taken leave of his senses, before being swept off her feet into his arms.

'Hey! What do you think you're doing. Put me down!'

'Madam. Look!'

From the shade of a tree she looked. And there it was. Coiled around the corner of the step. A long green mamba - one of Kenya's deadliest snakes. Two more seconds and she could have been on top of it.

'Once I got over the shock I was so thankful,' she wrote afterwards. 'Both to the man whose quick action saved me and to the people, who I know, pray faithfully for my personal safety day by day. God certainly answered their prayers.'

Yes, missionary life could be dangerous. At the same time, even after this incident, fear of the local wild-life was one thing which never kept Katie awake at night. Certainly from time to time she might discover a snake on her doorstep or a scorpion in the shower. But she knew the creatures would not strike unless they felt threatened. Basically, she understood, they meant her no harm.

The same could not be said for every human being she encountered. At the very time when things were going well - when so many children were recovering in the Children's Centre and everyone, from the most important official in the Ministry of Health to the poorest beggar in the village, was full of praise for the work - the missionary discovered something. Human revenge could be more dangerous and harder to deal with than the most poisonous reptile.

The last thing Katie had ever imagined was that she would make enemies of Gilbert and Rachel Rotich. Everything had been perfectly polite and friendly when they first came to Litein. Gilbert Rotich was the new headmaster of the local secondary school (situated 100 yards down the road from the Children's Centre) while his wife, Rachel, was a nurse.

'Are there any vacancies for staff in the Dispensary?' she had asked Katie at their first meeting.

'There certainly are.' Katie had offered her the position of staff nurse on the spot. 'Of course I'll have to check it through with the Dispensary Management Committee,' she added. 'But there shouldn't be any problem.' Nurses would never be short of a job.

Just as expected the Dispensary Management Committee approved the appointment and Rachel started work. Everything went smoothly until, one day, Katie arrived on the ward to find her new colleague about to give an injection.

'Hold on a moment - this patient is only supposed to get 5 mls of chloroquin,' she pointed out, noting that Rachel had 20 mls in the syringe.

If she expected the headmaster's wife to be apologetic, she was in for a nasty surprise. Rachel seemed more put out by the interference than by the fact that she had made a mistake.

'You must always be careful to give exactly the dosage on the chart,' Katie insisted as nicely, yet as firmly, as she could.

From that moment on their relationship turned sour. Rachel resented the reprimand. She became sullen and difficult to work with. When Katie was around she made a point of carefully measuring any medicine - but she did it with the air of an experienced cook suddenly being forced to weigh ingredients for the sake of some half-witted assistant.

The missionary suspected she was still doing things her own way behind her back. And finally she had proof. She walked in one morning to find Rachel about to give a second patient a dangerously high dose of a drug. This time there was no question of taking the staff nurse to one side. Katie simply snatched the syringe, emptied half its contents into a bowl and completed the injection herself.

Her authoritative action spoke louder than a thousand words. Rachel felt humiliated. She shot Katie a look of hatred, then turned on her heel and marched straight out of the Dispensary and down the road without saying when - if ever - she would be back.

That afternoon the whole affair was brought before the Dispensary Management Committee. Katie explained what had happened as well as she could, while the group of men listened in expressionless silence. Then, when she had finished, they asked her to make them some tea. It was as if they were simply sitting there, waiting for something to happen.

They didn't have to wait long. Half-way through the tea-drinking session Rotich strutted into the room.

For the next half-an-hour he laid down the law. As far as he was concerned everything was Katie's fault. It was quite impossible for his wife to work under someone so rude and overbearing. She had left and would only return to the Dispensary on one condition. The Committee must give the white missionary the sack.

What would happen now? The headmaster was an important figure in the local community. No management committee interested in good public relations would willingly offend him.

'We are indeed sorry to hear of your wife's difficulty,' the chairman said politely. 'But if these two nurses cannot work together happily, it is better that one should go.'

Sitting there at the back of the room, Katie experienced a wave of relief. Without exactly saying it in so many words, Pastor Philip had made it clear that her own position was unchanged.

But she had made a dangerous enemy.

A few mornings later she turned on the kitchen tap. The water came out in a brown trickle, then stopped. 'Oh no,' she thought. 'We must have a burst pipe.' She tracked down a plumber only to be told it was nothing of the sort. 'Your water's been turned off at the mains, Madam,' she was informed.

Suddenly Katie put two and two together. Where was their stop-cock located? At the water tank, which was maintained by the local secondary school. Who had a reason for turning off their water? The headmaster - Gilbert Rotich.

It took hours to get the water back on again. Of course Katie couldn't accuse Rotich directly of acting out of spite. But there was no mistaking the quietly malicious edge to his smile as he explained that the caretaker must have made a 'small mistake.'

To Katie's fury, there was another 'small mistake' a few days later, followed by another and another - all causing her the greatest imaginable inconvenience.

These ongoing water problems, however, were like a tickle in comparison to the blow which lay ahead.

Katie had a visit from some members of the Dispensary Management committee. One look at their faces was enough to tell her that it wasn't a social call.

'We have received a number of serious complaints,' they informed her. 'You have been accused of beating patients in the Dispensary.'

'Beating patients!' The whole thing sounded so ridiculous Katie almost smiled. But the visiting pastors were in deadly earnest.

'Just who has been saying this?' the missionary demanded.

'People, villagers.'

'Rotich and his friends,' Katie thought - although again she had no proof.

The next few weeks were amongst the most difficult in her life. The rumours had clearly spread through the community. 'No one has ever been able to tame the tongue. It is evil and uncontrollable, full of deadly poison,' the apostle James wrote (James 3:8). In those weeks the painful truth of his words came home in a new way.

The Dispensary Management Committee decided that the matter would have to be settled once and for all. 'We have arranged a public meeting with your accusers,' Katie was informed. 'We will hear what everyone has to say, then come to a decision.'

Katie came to that meeting knowing that her future hung in the balance. Hour after hour she sat listening to accusation after accusation. But in the end only one man came across in a convincing manner. He was someone whom Katie had never seen before in her life, yet he described in the fullest detail how she had almost beaten his mother to death. When Pastor Philemon (a deep-thinking, godly man) asked if he could recall when the incident had happened, he immediately supplied a time and date.

'Now Katie,' Pastor Philemon turned to the missionary. 'I want you to give me your passport.'

Her passport? What on earth did he want that for? Katie was so hurt and dispirited by the whole proceedings she couldn't begin to think.

Wearily she took the document out of her bag.

Pastor Philemon opened it, flicked through a few pages and smiled.

'There, my friend.' He handed the dark navy booklet with its gold embossed cover across to the missionary's accuser. 'Katie could not possibly have beaten your mother on the date you say.

According to the official stamp on this passport she was out of the country.'

A hole the size of an elephant had been poked at the centre of the most convincing story. From there on it was a simple matter to show that the other tales were equally untrue. To a man, the Dispensary Management Committee expressed total confidence in the character and ability of their missionary nurse. 'So let us give her every support and put all this unpleasantness behind us,' the chairman concluded.

'That's fine as far as I am concerned,' Katie thought, as she left the room. 'But what about Rotich?' If she had to cope with another series of water-cuts after the terrible strain of the past weeks, she felt sure she would crack.

She need not have worried. A few days after the hearing she received a most unusual communication in the post. It was a copy of a letter addressed to Rotich. 'I understand you have been opposing the missionary nurse in charge of Litein Dispensary,' it read. 'I also understand that your wife used to work in that Dispensary but is now no longer employed there.'

The signature at the bottom belonged to a well-known Member of Parliament. It was followed by a long list of names. 'Copy sent to X, copy sent to Y, copy sent to Z...' Everyone who was anyone, apparently, had received a copy of this letter:

Church leaders, Mission leaders, Government Health Officials, Educational Officers - the list was endless.

Slowly Katie sank into a seat, the letter clasped between her hands. She felt the same mixture of shock and deep thankfulness that she had felt after her sudden deliverance from the venom of a poisonous snake. She knew there was no way Rotich could continue to oppose her now that so many people had been put wise to his little game. Her reputation was safe. Her work could continue. Once again, at a time of very great danger, the Lord had intervened.

11
BLESSINGS

A few months after the M.P.'s letter, Rotich was unexpectedly moved from Litein.

'I suppose I should be surprised,' Katie told Matthew when she heard the news. 'But I'm not.'

Matthew considered. 'It's as if God isn't going to allow anything to stand in the way of this work,' he said slowly. 'Anyone who opposes it walks into trouble.'

'That's right,' Katie nodded. She was reminded of a verse from the book of Genesis - God's words to Abraham: 'I will bless those who bless you. But I will curse those who curse you' (Gen 12:3). Yes, the God whom she served was a God of love but he was also a God of judgment; and the beginnings of his judgments - his punishments and blessings - could often be seen on earth.

Happily she was much more conscious of people being blessed through their involvement with the Children's Centre than the other way round. Over the years she had heard of so many answers to prayer in her supporters' lives. There had been material blessings such as food, clothes, houses, cars, jobs; spiritual blessings such as happy homes and peaceful hearts; and many examples of that greatest blessing of all - the gift of the right partner in life.

Katie stored up all these stories in her heart. Then, when the young nurses from the Dispensary would come to see her with their boyfriend troubles, she knew exactly how to give them the encouragement they needed.

Often she would begin by telling the story of Esther - a girl who had worked in the Dispensary.

Esther was a Christian with one main aim in life; she wanted to please God. Her faith made her one of the brightest, most caring nurses on the wards. Katie often noticed how she went out of her way to make the patients comfortable and cheer them up.

One day a woman came into the Dispensary from a village on the other side of the Mau forest. Because she had come so far, she had come on her own which meant she had no-one to prepare her meals. (Hospitals in rural Kenya only supplied treatment, not food.) Esther noticed this. Typically, without saying anything to anyone, she began to share her food. Day after day she would carry a plate full of maize and beans to the woman's bed, and stay chatting to her while she ate.

About a week after the woman's admission, someone came to see her. How her eyes lit up as this particular visitor strode into the ward! Here he was at last - her strong, handsome son. He had left his work and made the long journey to find out how she was getting on. Naturally the first person she wanted him to meet was Esther. 'Come. Come and see the one who has been like a daughter to me,' she dragged the young man half-way round the Dispensary in her eagerness to make the introduction.

It was a case of love at first sight. No sooner had the son set eyes on Esther's lovely smiling face than he fell for her in a big way. Esther felt exactly the same about him, and by the time the woman was well enough to leave the Dispensary their marriage had been arranged.

As far as Katie was concerned she had watched the whole romance with the greatest delight. She knew, from her reading of Scripture, that God had promised to reward his children for every caring action they performed. And now she felt she was seeing the beginning of Esther's reward. She was also reminded of the Biblical story of Boaz and Ruth. There too a young woman had gone the second mile to take care of an older one, and there too, the path of loving-kindness had taken her straight into the arms of her God-given partner in life.

Another girl the missionary often talked about was Betty. Betty had been a volunteer with Campus Crusade and had come to Litein to work for a year. It quickly became clear that when it came to caring she, too, was always ready to go the second mile. As soon as she had finished duty in the Dispensary, she would nip across to the Children's Centre. 'Anything I can do to help?' she would call as she appeared in Katie's door.

With some people it was so much trouble to show them what to do, it was easier for Katie to finish the job herself. Betty wasn't like that. She was one of the most practical creatures who ever lifted a spoon. Sewing, baking, cleaning cupboards, changing nappies - you name it, Betty was ready and able to take it on. More than once Katie looked at the slim, curly-haired figure with her quick hands and bright smile and marvelled at the difference she could make to the house in a few short minutes.

Shortly after Betty's arrival, a doctor friend from Kijabe Hospital came to pay the Dispensary a call. He was accompanied by a fair-haired young Canadian called Grant. Before Katie had even finished making them coffee, Grant had made himself at home. With Kipngeno on one knee and Chebet on the other, he looked as if he'd been a regular visitor for years.

The doctor took the opportunity to take Katie to one side and explain a little more about his companion. To Katie's surprise, the story was a sad one: Grant was about to go blind. 'He has very serious diabetes and over the past year his sight has been rapidly deteriorating,' the doctor explained. The young man's relatives had decided to send him for a holiday in Kenya so he could see the scenery and the animals while he still had the chance.

Suddenly Katie had an idea. There was an empty house on the mission station. Litein was a very beautiful area, and Grant obviously loved children. There and then she made up her mind. She would ask the fair-haired Canadian if he would like to stay for a while.

'Like to. I'd love it,' was Grant's eager response.

And so it was arranged. Grant became a temporary member of the Children's Centre family.

Katie had made the offer without expecting anything in return, but she was soon to discover that her guest had a different view of the matter. Like Betty, Grant was extremely practical. Within a few days of settling in, he had tackled the Children's Centre garden - digging and pruning and planting to the extent that Katie guessed it would probably produce twice as much of everything the following year.

Betty, meanwhile, was in and out of the house as usual. It became her habit to stop in the garden for a chat with Grant en route. As the days went by Katie noticed something; there was a particular glow about her resident handyman whenever the young nurse was around.

It caused her no great astonishment then, when he finally spoke of his feelings. All was just as she suspected. Grant loved Betty and knew of no person in the wide world that he would rather have for a wife. But - and it was a very big but - would any girl consider marrying a man who was about to go blind?

Katie saw the mixture of hope and despair in his eyes as he talked. 'Listen, Grant, Betty isn't "any girl",' she said gently. 'We both know she's special. So you just keep praying about this. And so will I.'

Surprise! Surprise! The next person to look for a private chat with Katie was Betty herself.

'I've been thinking about Grant,' she began shyly.

'Have you?' the missionary smiled.

'You know it seems to me that his health would be better if he took more care of himself and ate proper food at the right times.'

'You've got something there,' Katie nodded. She too had noticed that Grant was often careless about his diet.'

'So I was wondering...' Betty hesitated. 'I mean, do you think he'd mind if I started cooking his meals?' The words came out in a rush.

The missionary's smile became a very broad

grin. 'Mind! I think he'd be delighted.' she said.

There was a permanent glow about Grant from then on. Not only had he never been so well fed, but his cook seemed perfectly prepared to take the job on for life. When he had asked how she felt about his future blindness, she said that it made no difference. She loved him, and as far as future problems were concerned, well, she was prepared to leave them with God.

Before the month was out the couple had announced their engagement.

And then - trouble!

'We would like to get married this summer,' Betty explained to her Mission.

'Out of the question. You're committed to a full year's service!' she was told.

'Just keep praying. Ask God to show you his will,' Katie comforted.

So they prayed on - and the more they prayed, the more certain they became that an early wedding was right. Thanks to Betty's care and plenty of exercise in the Children's Centre garden, Grant's general health had improved, but his vision was still worsening. It made sense - and in the end even Betty's Mission had to admit this - that the couple should marry while the groom could still see his bride walk down the aisle.

But God had a further surprise in store.

A few months after the wedding, Katie received a very excited letter from Betty. A Canadian health organization had been looking for someone with poor sight to take part in an experiment using a new laser therapy. Grant had volunteered. 'We don't know what effect the laser will have on his eyes, but we have nothing to lose,' she finished. 'Please pray that it will be helpful.'

If this letter was excited, the one which came the following month was exuberant. In sentence after sentence Betty poured out her joy. The laser treatment had helped more than anyone dared hope. Their worries were over. The miracle had happened. Grant wasn't going blind after all!

'So you see,' Katie would remind her listeners at the end of the story. 'It is always best for us to leave the future in God's hands. He has promised that if we make pleasing him our main aim in life, he will take care of all the rest (Matthew 6:33): food, clothes, money, health - even husbands.

The girls would nod. 'Ah yes, Katie. We see that,' they would smile.

Sometimes though, she could sense an unspoken question in the air.

'What about you? God has given you no husband. Are you not sad?'

The simple answer was no. Right at the very beginning of her missionary career Katie had heard God ask if she was willing to remain single for his sake and she had said 'yes'.

It was a reply she had never regretted.

Certainly she had seen many wonderful blessings in the lives of her friends and co-workers. But here, in Litein, she had people supporting her work in all corners of Scotland and beyond. She had her house full of bright-eyed children and a huge loving community on her doorstep. Sad? How could she be sad?

'I have been blessed more than anyone,' she would say.

12
A BAD BEGINNING

Although Katie was so happy in Litein, both in her work and in her many friendships, the time eventually came for her to move on. During a period of ill-health two things had become clear. First, she needed to go home to Scotland for a rest and second (fortunately under the circumstances!) she had worked herself out of a job; Matthew and Priscilla were now quite capable of looking after the Children's Centre on their own.

There was huge lump in her throat at her farewell party. It was so very hard to say goodbye. On behalf of the whole village Matthew presented her with a mat of black and white goatskins sewn closely together. 'This mat is a Kipsigis symbol of motherhood,' he explained. 'We give it to you because you have been a mother to many of our children. We also give it as a sign of the wonderful closeness we share in the Lord.'

Three days later, with this precious gift carefully stowed away in her suitcase, Katie made her way through the baggage check-out at Glasgow airport.

'Katie!' Her heart leapt at the sound of familiar voices on the other side of the barrier - the voices of her parents, sister and brother-in-law.

'Oh, it's just great to see you!'

'It's great to see you too.'

The pain of her recent goodbyes faded as Katie wheeled her trolley towards their car. Yes, she had left her dear Kipsigis family behind. But she had her own dear family to return to. Rona and Jessie were married now with children of their own. 'I'm sure I'll hardly recognize them - they'll have grown so much,' she exclaimed happily.

It was good to be home. Good to taste her Mum's Scottish oatcake - good to listen to her Dad's stories - good to catch up on all the family news - good to read library books in the peace of her own room.

But as well as being a time to relax, this year in Scotland was also a time for Katie to talk about her work. She had so many invitations to speak at meetings, she could have been out every night of the week. All sorts of groups had heard about the Kipsigis children and wanted to know how they were getting on.

'The wonderful thing is that the Church now sees the special need of children whose parents have died,' Katie would explain. 'It isn't just Kipsigis children who are being helped. All over the country new Children's Centres are springing up.'

'So what will you be doing when you go back?'

was usually the next question.

'More children's work,' she would reply. 'But I'm not quite sure where.'

At that stage it didn't seem to matter. She felt sure that just as God had guided her to Litein through the decision of the Mission authorities, so he would continue to guide when they came to decide about her new assignment.

In the meantime she was making the most of the chance to meet with so many people - particularly those under twelve. She quickly lost count of the number of schools she had visited. The interest of the pupils never failed to amaze her. Often they would decide on the spot to raise money for her work. All sorts of projects resulted: street fairs, concerts, sales of work. And then there were the individual efforts - like the little girl who made perfume out of rose petals and another eight-year-old who bred stick insects and sold them as pets!

But the effort which Katie found most moving took place in the school in Lochgilphead - her own home town. The children there had been amongst the first to see her slides.

'We would like to have a sale to buy equipment for the Children's Centre,' they told their headmaster.

'That's fine. But it has to be your own work,' he replied.

Like all the rest of the teachers, he thought they

would only raise a small sum.

He was in for a shock. Instead of turning up with the old comics, marbles and jigsaws with pieces missing which he had expected, the pupils arrived in with some of their very best toys. One lad, who lived in a children's home himself, actually insisted in placing his only possession - a large, rather moth-eaten teddy-bear - on the stall.

Katie could have cried when she heard.

'They were willing to part with things they would really miss,' the headmaster told her. He enclosed in his letter a cheque for a staggering one hundred and twenty pounds.

There was just one pupil who wasn't altogether thrilled with her school's achievement. And that was Jane, Katie's seven-year-old niece. Jane was bright. She could add. She could write. She knew what things cost. But only the older classes had been allowed to help with the sale. She hadn't been given the chance to put a price tag on one single toy, let alone take in the money and give change.

'It isn't fair!' she told her mother tearfully. 'I could have sold things better than anyone. Especially when it was for my own aunt!'

Rona smiled. 'I'll tell you what. You can have a sale here. We'll do a bit of baking between now and Saturday and then set up a stall outside the house.'

Jane instantly cheered up. 'That's a brilliant

idea. I'll get some of my friends to help. We could make toffee and crispies buns, and we could sell juice too.'

It was the beginning of a very busy week. By the end of it Jane felt she knew all there was to know about organizing sales. From where she stood, behind her white-clothed table, she could see a crowd of friends and neighbours already gathering outside the gate. The table was piled high with things to sell - toys, books, home-made sweets and cakes. She even had a couple of extra trays of toffee in reserve.

At two o'clock sharp the gate was opened. The crowd surged in. And the next minute business was booming. Jane and her helpers could hardly put things into bags quickly enough to keep up with the demand.

'Jane!' a friend called from her end of the table. 'The toffee's all gone. Did you say there was more?'

'Yes. It's here - under the table.'

The girl knelt down.

'Oh no! Mum! Look!' A maddening sight met her eyes. Instead of two trays full of shining brown toffee ready to be cut up and sold, she found two trays full of little brown chippings and her two-year-old brother Gavin chewing happily alongside an equally sticky small friend.

Only Rona's speedy arrival on the scene saved

the culprits from being hauled out by the hair.

'I spent ages making that toffee, and now Angus and Gavin have eaten the whole lot,' Jane wailed.

'What a shame,' the surrounding neighbours murmured sympathetically, and proceeded to hand out large sums for every rubbishy item in sight to cheer her up.

Needless to say the sale was a wonderful success.

It was June by this time - the month Katie was due to return to Kenya. She was spending her last few weeks in Scotland quietly with her Mum and Dad. One thing she had promised to do, though, was to show her slides in the local village hall the day before she left.

'I'll be sitting in the front row, Auntie Katie,' Jane promised.

But to Katie's surprise when the day came her niece was nowhere to be seen - not in the front row, nor the second row, nor anywhere else in the hall. Stranger still, her sister Rona was missing too.

Was something wrong? Could one of the family have taken ill?

Just as the missionary was about to begin speaking, a neighbour slipped up to the platform and handed her a note.

Oh no! The colour drained from her face as she read it. Jane had been taken to hospital.

As soon as politeness allowed Katie sped home to find out exactly what had happened.

Jane, it turned out, had been on her way to the meeting with a friend. Realizing that she was a little late, she had started to run. In her hurry, she hadn't noticed the leafy branch overhanging her path. A twig had pierced her eye.

'There's some fear she may lose it,' Katie's mum explained. 'The doctor sent her straight to the eye hospital in Glasgow.'

Katie's first thought was to go straight there herself, but her parents quickly scuppered that idea. It would be a wasted journey. There was nothing she could do. And in any case she still had a hundred and one things to sort out before her return flight to Kenya.

Kenya! The thought of the air-ticket in her handbag now filled the missionary with dismay. How could she leave at a time like this?

Even as she was wondering what to do, Jane was being wheeled into theatre. For hour after hour the surgeons fought to save her eye. Finally, though, they had to admit defeat.

'Everything that could be done was done,' Rona told Katie sadly on the phone. 'Still we can be thankful that she has come through the operation so well. As far as your departure to Kenya goes, there's absolutely no point in any delay.'

So Katie went. But never had leaving home

proved more difficult. Never had her heart been so heavy as she stepped onto the plane. It was as if all her joy in God's service had been drained away, drop by drop, in the long hours her niece had lain on that operating table.

'I'll feel different once I get back to work,' she told herself firmly. In the past she had always found that working with children - treating them, feeding them, cuddling them - was the very best cure for homesickness.

It never entered her head that the Mission might have some other kind of assignment in mind. But that was the bombshell which awaited her when she reported to the Church Office two days later.

'You are being assigned to Mulango Dispensary in the Kitui region,' the personnel official informed her. 'It has been shut for two years and the Church Leaders there want it reopened.'

Katie gasped. How had this happened? God had called her to work with children, hadn't he? The last thing she wanted to do was spend her days working in an outpatient Dispensary.

She reached Mulango to find she wouldn't even have that satisfaction. No-one suffering from anything would be coming to Mulango Dispensary for a very long time. The mud-brick building, with its corrugated iron roof, had been taken over by wild-life. Bats - thousands of them - had made their home in the rafters, soaking the ceiling with urine, while down below the medical records had been half-eaten by termites.

Almost sickened by the smell, the missionary lurched out into the open and leant against a car. Ever since Jane's accident she had been feeling low, but now her spirits hit rock bottom. Was this what she had left home for? To spend the next six weeks cleaning out this dreadful place and scrounging around for medicines?

She was confused. She was angry.

Somebody somewhere seemed to have made a terrible mistake.

God surely hadn't intended to send her here.

13

THE ANSWER IS 'NO'

Jane made an excellent recovery from her operation. Soon she was back at school where she seemed to manage every bit as well with one eye as her class-mates did with two.

'It's amazing the way she has got used to it,' Rona told Katie.

Katie was greatly relieved to hear this good news. Unfortunately, though, she couldn't say the same about her own situation.

On the outside things had progressed. She had cleaned out the Dispensary, borrowed medicines from Kijabe Hospital, and the building was now open and being run by two capable Akamba women. She had also discovered that her new assignment was not intended to stop her doing children's work, after all. 'I wanted the Dispensary opened in Mulango because the Church Leaders there have been requesting it for so long,' the Bishop had explained. 'But I know you always work with children, so that is exactly what I want you to do.'

By the end of October the babies had started to arrive. Philip, John, Mutuo and Musembi had taken over Katie's spare bedroom just as Kipngeno,

Chepkirui, Kipkoech, Kipkirui and Chebet had done in Litein.

Yes, outward progress had been made. But inside Katie still nursed a great deal of bitterness and pain.

Part of the problem was that she was lonely. In Litein there had been a steady stream of visitors in and out of her house - nurses, members of the Dispensary Management Committee, people from the local church. They had all taken an interest in the children and treated Katie as one of themselves. But in Mulango she was lucky to have a caller from one week to the next. Somehow she couldn't seem to make a single friend.

It wasn't that she hadn't tried. It was more that the Akamba people just didn't seem to realize she needed company. In fact they didn't seem to think she had any needs or feelings at all.

There was the time she had offered four neighbours a lift to Nairobi, for example. She had been looking forward to the trip. 'We'll be able to have a really good chat in the car,' she thought happily.

Sure enough there was plenty of conversation throughout that three and half hour journey. But Katie might as well have travelled on the roof-rack. Her companions (who all spoke good English) had chatted amongst themselves in their own Kikamba language - of which she understood not one word - from the moment they left Mulango until the moment the car pulled into a petrol station on the outskirts of the city.

By this stage the missionary was feeling so hurt and left out she was ready to explode.

'See that cafe over there,' she pointed across the road. 'Well, after I've paid for the petrol I'm going in there for a cup of coffee. And if any of you want to join me, you're welcome.'

Her four passengers were already sitting down with their coffee and a plate of cakes apiece when she arrived in the tea-room. They hadn't got anything for her. But they had let the cashier know she was coming.

'What!' Katie gasped when she got her bill. 'You can't possibly be charging that amount for one cup of coffee!'

'Indeed no, madam,' the cashier smiled. 'Your friends also had coffee and cakes. And they said you would pay.'

That one incident summed up the attitude Katie felt the Akamba people had towards her. They seemed to see her not as a someone to get to know, but as someone to get things from.

Of course, once she had simmered down, she could understand why. Mulango was at the heart of the Kitui region, an area of 12,000 square miles of very poor land. When the rains came, the crops grew and people had food to put on the table. But often the rains failed and life became a simple battle for survival. It was hard for people used to living like that to see white missionaries as anything other than wealthy westerners, able to dip their hands in their pockets whenever they felt inclined.

Yes, Katie could understand why the local people should see her like that, and she could forgive them for it. What she found much harder to forgive was their attitude towards the sick or orphaned babies they brought to her home. 'Does no-one care what happens to them once they are inside my door?' she often wondered - as she sat visitorless in the nursery for the umpteenth day in a row.

December came - and she prepared to write her first prayer letter from Mulango. By this stage she had eleven babies in the house.

'I don't want this to sound like one long moan,' she reminded herself as she lifted her pen. She searched her mind for something positive to say. It wasn't easy. The only thing plentiful around here is germs, she thought. I don't have enough water. I don't have any African friends. And I still suspect God has made a big mistake sending me here.

She did her best to put a brave face on it. 'The children are, as usual, a very great joy and we have watched God at work healing wee, sick bodies,' she wrote in the end.

But there was no way she could have put a brave face on the events of the following weeks.

Suddenly, at the beginning of what she had hoped would be a happy New Year, almost every child in the house fell ill. And this time it wasn't just the usual tummy troubles. They had coughs, fevers, chicken pox, measles and no sooner did they seem to be recovering from one infection than they came down with something else. Hour after hour, night after night Katie was up taking temperatures, giving drinks, ice-baths, injections; every treatment she could think of to make the babies better.

Despite all her efforts four of them had died. Even then the Church Leaders didn't set foot in the house.

This heartbreak brought the long months of unhappiness to a head. The missionary was now completely convinced that Mulango was not her special place. How could God want me to stay here with such uncaring leaders? she reasoned. Through the long night hours, she lay awake making imaginary plans. As soon as the children were stronger - as soon as the arrangements could be made - she would pack up bag and baggage, and move her whole household elsewhere.

But first, after all the upset of the past few months, she knew she needed a break. Even before the children had taken sick she had been hoping to spend a few days away from Mulango.

'Don't worry. We'll keep an eye on things here,' her fellow missionaries promised.

So Katie put her Bible, a few clothes and her wash-things into an overnight bag and set off for a quiet Christian Guest House in Limuru.

The next morning she was up early, but, to the landlady's surprise she didn't appear for breakfast. She didn't bother with lunch either, nor with dinner that night. It had been so long since she had had time alone with God, that she had decided to devote herself to prayer. Normally, she might have found it hard to fast like that, but on this occasion she was seeking God's will with such urgency, it seemed to take away any desire for food.

She wanted to move. But where should she go? She felt desperately in need of God's guidance on the matter.

So she prayed on. The hours passed. And gradually she knew with complete certainty that she was hearing the deep inner voice of God's Spirit. She had her answer - but it brought her no relief. The message went against everything she had hoped and planned.

God was telling her to 'stay put'.

'But how can I stay in Mulango?' she argued. 'I just can't cope with the loneliness anymore. Please let me move somewhere else.'

Even as she asked she had the sense of God's loving arms around her, comforting her, assuring her that she need never feel alone while he was by her side.

But still, his instruction remained the same as before. The answer to her heart-felt request was 'no'.

14
A FRIEND IN FAMINE

The sun was just beginning to lose its blistering mid-afternoon heat when Katie reached her destination. 'How brown and scorched everything looks,' she thought as she strolled towards the pastor's bungalow. She knocked on the door.

'Anyone at home?' Her face lit up as an elderly grey-haired African stepped outside in response to her call.

'Ah, Katie!' He shook her warmly by the hand.

'How are you today, Reverend Konzi?'

'I am fine, fine. And you?'

'I'm well too. Have you time for a chat?'

Gone were the days when no Church Leader took an interest in Katie's work. 'You know I have always time for that,' the old man beamed.

Almost five years had passed since Katie had asked God to let her leave Mulango. She was still there. But she could now see how her loving Father had said 'no' to one request in order to say 'yes' to something much more exciting. A move had taken place - five kilometres down the road to Kitui town. Even now when Katie walked through the front door of her new living-quarters she felt a thrill of gratitude. This Baby Home was a dream come true - a purpose-built building, big enough to cater comfortably for over fifty children. It had cost over £30,000 to build, and every penny of that huge sum had come flooding into her bank account in answer to prayer.

But what meant more to the missionary than anything else had been the Reverend Konzi's help and advice. Ever since this wise old African with his sparkling sense of humour had taken over as Chairman of the Regional Church Council, Katie had had all the support she needed.

It was Rev. Konzi who had negotiated with the government to obtain a plot of land on which the new Baby Home could be built. It was Rev. Konzi who had found staff to help Katie with the children. It was Rev. Konzi who came to read the Bible and pray with her when the children were sick. And most important, it was Rev. Konzi who liked nothing better than a long relaxing chat over a cup of coffee.

They always had so much to talk about - Baby Home matters, family matters, health matters. Today, though, their main topic of conversation was the weather.

Usually this was the last thing any African would discuss. The weather was totally predictable. Every day was dry and sunny, except for a spell in December and another in April when the heavens opened and rain poured down on to the thirsty earth. The problem was that this year the April rains were late - so late that the water pipes to the Baby Home had gone dry.

'We've had to send for the water lorry,' Katie told Rev. Konzi. 'And all the plants in the garden are dead. It's so annoying.'

Her friend nodded sympathetically. 'We must pray that the rains will come soon,' he said.

Weeks went by - long dry weeks. The water lorry was in such demand, it was sometimes well after dark before it reached the Baby Home. People stopped saying: 'Any day now we will have rain.' Their expectancy had been replaced by resignation. All the mugginess had disappeared from the atmosphere. They knew this meant the rainy season had passed, and the rains had not come.

Nothing grew in the fields that year - no beans, no peas, no cabbages, maize or broccoli. With no fresh vegetables, the villagers tried to make their small stores of dried food last as long as possible. October came, and the women went out with their hoes to dig up the sun-baked earth. Hope rose in their hearts as they planted new seeds to replace the ones which had rotted in the ground. Soon it would be December and the sky would become cloudy again. Surely this time the rains would fall.

But they didn't.

Instead women and children started coming in

very large numbers to the Baby Home door. The children were painfully thin, and their mothers were even thinner. For months they had been surviving on one inadequate meal a day, and now they had completely run out of food.

Katie could only take in the very worst cases...children like little Kilonzo, who had been carried to the Home by the headmaster of his school.

'He had been missing from class for a number of weeks,' the man explained. 'So I called at his house to see what had happened. I found Kilonzo alone on a mat, too weak to move. It looked as if he'd been there for days.'

'His mother must have left him to search for food and died before she could return,' said Katie sadly, taking the little boy into her arms.

Tragedies like this were common during a time of famine.

Knowing how desperately needy the people were, the missionary tried never to send anyone away from her door empty-handed. Together with Rev. Konzi, she drew up a list of all the poorest family groups in the area. 'Come to the Baby Home once a week from now on,' she would instruct her callers. 'And we will pray that God will send enough food so that you and your family will have something to eat.'

So week by week the people came, waiting in

ever-lengthening queues, for the rations of rice and beans that would keep them alive. It tore at Katie's heart to see them there - so thin, weak and patient. Yet even in the middle of her distress there were moments of laughter.

One week she had noticed an old beggar lady staggering though Kitui town on the verge of collapse. She had brought her back to the Baby Home and given her a meal. A few days later the same lady had returned to her door, with four bent wrinkled companions - all equally desperate for food. Katie sat them down under a tree in the garden, sent them out bowls of rice and continued with her own work inside. Twenty minutes later she was informed that the beggars wished to see her before leaving. To her surprise she found all five of them standing to attention in a straight line. With great ceremony the lady number one took hold of Katie's hand and formally spat in her palm. Number two did the same and number three, and so on down the row. Then, having expressed their thanks in the traditional Akamban manner, her visitors departed, leaving Katie with a very broad grin on her face, and a very messy palm.

April came and went with hardly a cloud in the sky. Food was in such short supply that people must have found it impossible to remember what full tummies felt like. 'The famine is awful. The families of the children who are now better are all struggling to stay alive. There is no prospect of sending them home,' one of Katie's helpers wrote at that time.

Somehow the Baby Home managed to stay afloat on this sea of need. By October eighty children had been squeezed in under its roof and around 700 people were being fed from its store-room. (These included Katie's five beggar ladies who continued to thank her in their own special way after each meal.)

There were times when Katie hardly knew from one meal to the next where the food would come from. As an official Distribution Centre, the Home was supposed to receive regular deliveries of basic supplies. But sometimes, especially after the rains failed for the third time, the Famine Relief lorries did not appear. 'Lord, please help me not to send anyone away hungry from this door,' she would pray. And again and again God answered her prayer. Just as in the early days he had faithfully provided for her family of five, so now he continued to show that he could exactly meet the needs of the huge Baby Home commu-nity.

Never did Katie see this more clearly than the week they almost ran out of sugar.

For almost a month she had watched her stocks of the stuff dwindle with growing concern. She had done her best to get more. Sugar was such an important part of her sick children's diet. It gave them the energy their weak malnourished stomachs could not accept in any other form. But at the height of the famine it was as scarce as green grass. No matter how far she travelled, or who she asked, the reply was the same: 'Sugar? Sorry, we don't have any in to sell.'

'I'll have to look for honey instead,' the missionary decided on the day she took her last kilo of sugar out of the store. Raw honey, she knew, would be reasonably easy to come by. But her heart sank at the thought of the amount of work involved before she could feed it to the children. It would have to be boiled and strained and rebottled - a long, messy process. 'When will I ever have time for that?' she wondered wearily.

The answer was - never. At two o'clock that afternoon a lorry pulled up outside the Home. It wasn't a famine relief lorry, so Katie didn't associate it with food. Probably some driver looking for directions, she thought as she went to answer the door. What a surprise to find a group of smiling young people on her doorstep!

'Hello. We're from *Youth With A Mission*,' their spokesperson announced. 'We've brought some milk powder for the children.'

'Well, that's really very kind of you,' Katie beamed. She already had milk-powder, but food of any kind was welcome.

Five fifty kilo sacks of milk powder were promptly unloaded from the lorry, followed by a carton of salt, a carton of soap, a carton of matches and seventy-two bags of flour.

'Look. There's another sack away in there underneath that seat,' the driver pointed out as the last of the goods was carted into the Home.

Katie held her breath. Would it be...could it be...?

The driver went and gave the sack a kick. 'Sugar!' he pronounced casually, heaving the sack out. 'We might as well leave that here too.'

'He must have got a bit of a shock to turn round and find me almost in tears,' Katie told Rev. Konzi afterwards. 'I could hardly believe my eyes - so much sugar - just landing in our storeroom. I didn't know whether to laugh or cry.'

'Our God is good,' the old African nodded. He knew better than anyone what the people were going through. But he remained one of the most encouraging visitors to the Home. Often when Katie felt downhearted at the extent of the suffering around her, he helped her see afresh that God was in control. Only that afternoon he had come round with the wonderful news that Kilonzo's mother was still alive. 'You cannot imagine her joy when she heard that we had kept her son safe and well,' he smiled.

Yes, God was good. All through that long

drawn-out period of famine the missionary clung to that belief. Food was being supplied. Children were being saved. And finally one morning, she woke up to the glorious sound of rain pelting down on to the Baby Home roof. Was it just an isolated cloud-burst? No, day after day it persisted - steadily, heavily, penetrating deep into the ground.

After three weeks the sky cleared. With a thrill of delight Katie stepped out into her garden. A miraculous transformation had taken place. The earth which had been brown, bare and dreary was now a brilliant mass of colour. Grass grew. Trees blossomed. It was like stepping into another world. Beautiful exotic desert flowers, only seen after a period of drought, blazed in every corner.

Appreciatively she sniffed the perfumed air, drinking in the loveliness of it all. And as she stood there, she heard God speak. 'This is the transformation I make in the lives of my children,' he seemed to remind her. 'Even in the darkest times I am at work.'

Joy bubbled in Katie's heart, spilling out in words she had thought she could never say: 'Lord, your will for my life is perfect in every detail,' she whispered. 'Thank you for saying ''no'' when I wanted to leave Mulango. I'm so glad I was able to stay here and help people during the famine. Thank you for being with me in every experience.

'Thank you most of all for being my friend.'